HOPEFULLY YOU'RE ABOUT TO READ "LORNA." THIS IS JUST THE FIRST BOOK. SO I HOPE YOU STICK AROUND FOR THE FUTURE LORNA BOOKS!

LORNA, THE CHARACTER, WAS INSPIRED BY A GIRL I KNEW NAMED LORNA. DURING ELEMENTARY SCHOOL IN MISSOURI. SHE TAUGHT ME WHAT A BLOW-JOB WAS SO I WASN'T CONFUSED BY HER DIRTY JOKES. THE CHARACTER WAS ALSO VAGUELY INSPIRED BY A CASHIER AT OUR LOCAL GROCERY STORE AND SOME OF MY FAVORITE CHARACTERS FROM MY FAVORITE OLD HORROR/COMEDY MANGA.

SILVER SPROCKET
AVI EHRLICH – PUBLISHER
JOSH PM – GENERAL MANAGER
CARINA TAYLOR – PRODUCTION DESIGNER
NATALYE CHILDRESS – COPYEDITOR

LORNA © 2021 BENJI NATE. SECOND PRINTING, WINTER 2021.
PUBLISHED BY SILVER SPROCKET. NO PORTION OF THIS BOOK
(EXCEPT SMALL PORTIONS FOR REVIEW PURPOSES) MAY BE REPRODUCED IN ANY
FORM WITHOUT WRITTEN PERMISSION FROM THE AUTHOR OR PUBLISHER.
ALL RIGHTS RESERVED. PRINTED IN CANADA. ISBN: 978-1-945509-34-6

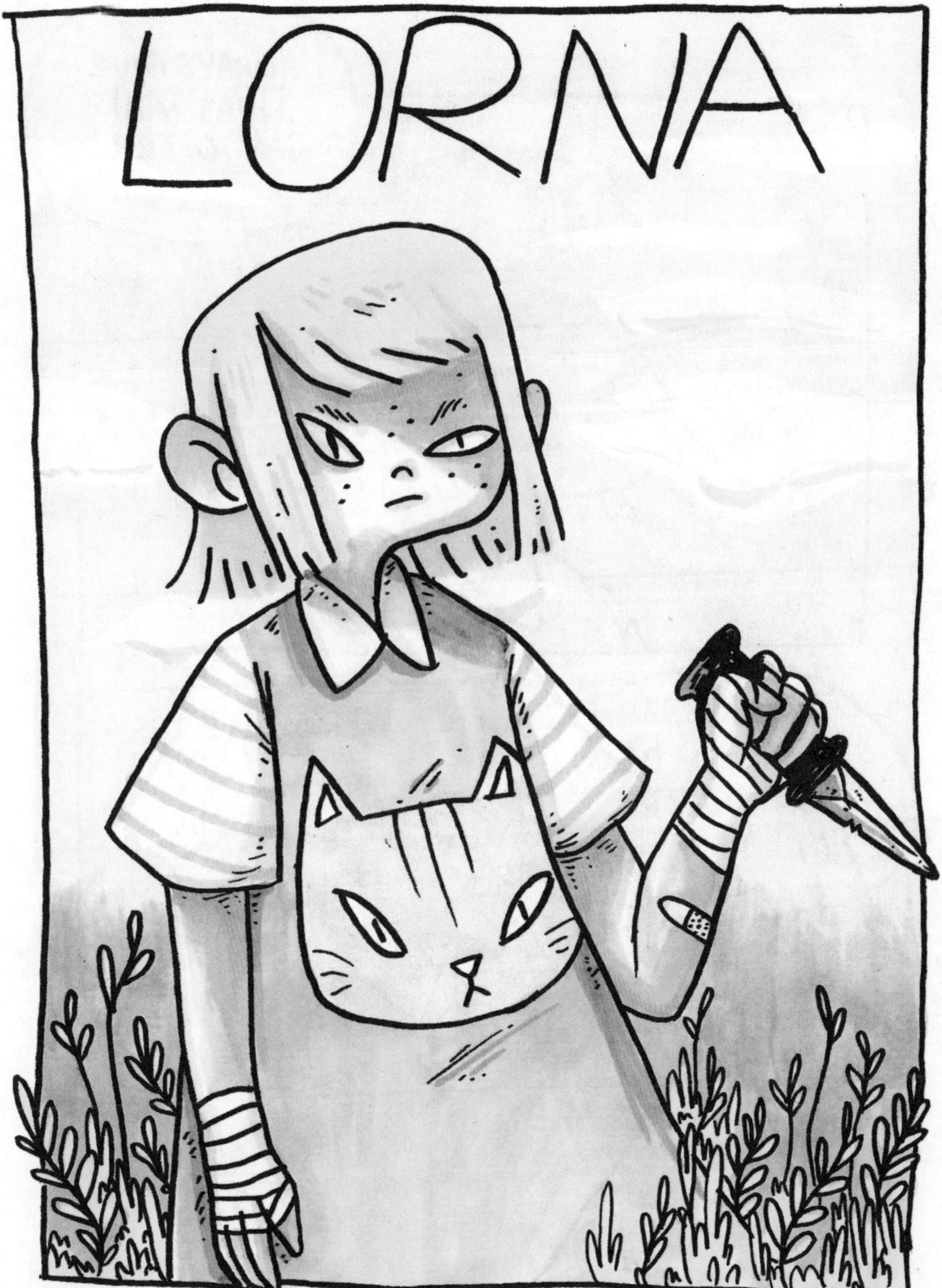
LORNA

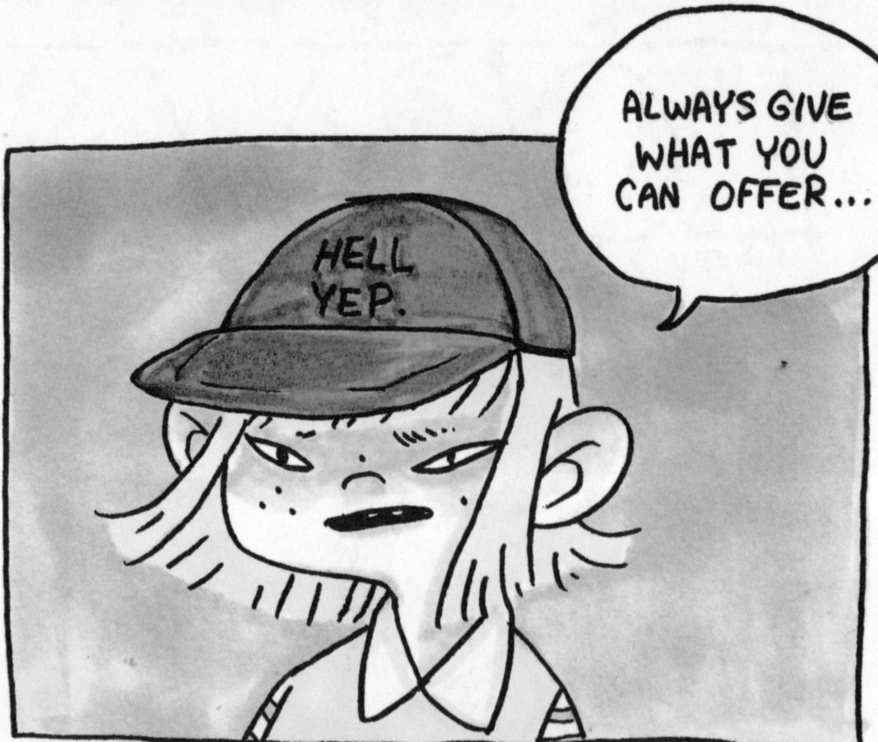
ALWAYS GIVE WHAT YOU CAN OFFER...
HELL YEP.

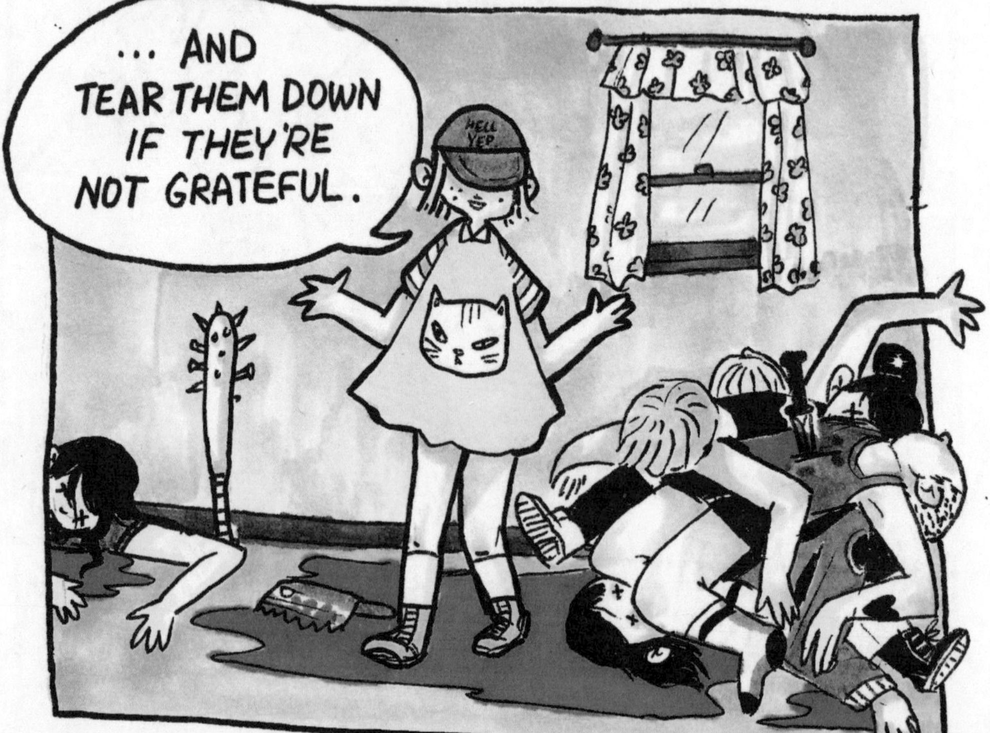
... AND TEAR THEM DOWN IF THEY'RE NOT GRATEFUL.
HELL YEP

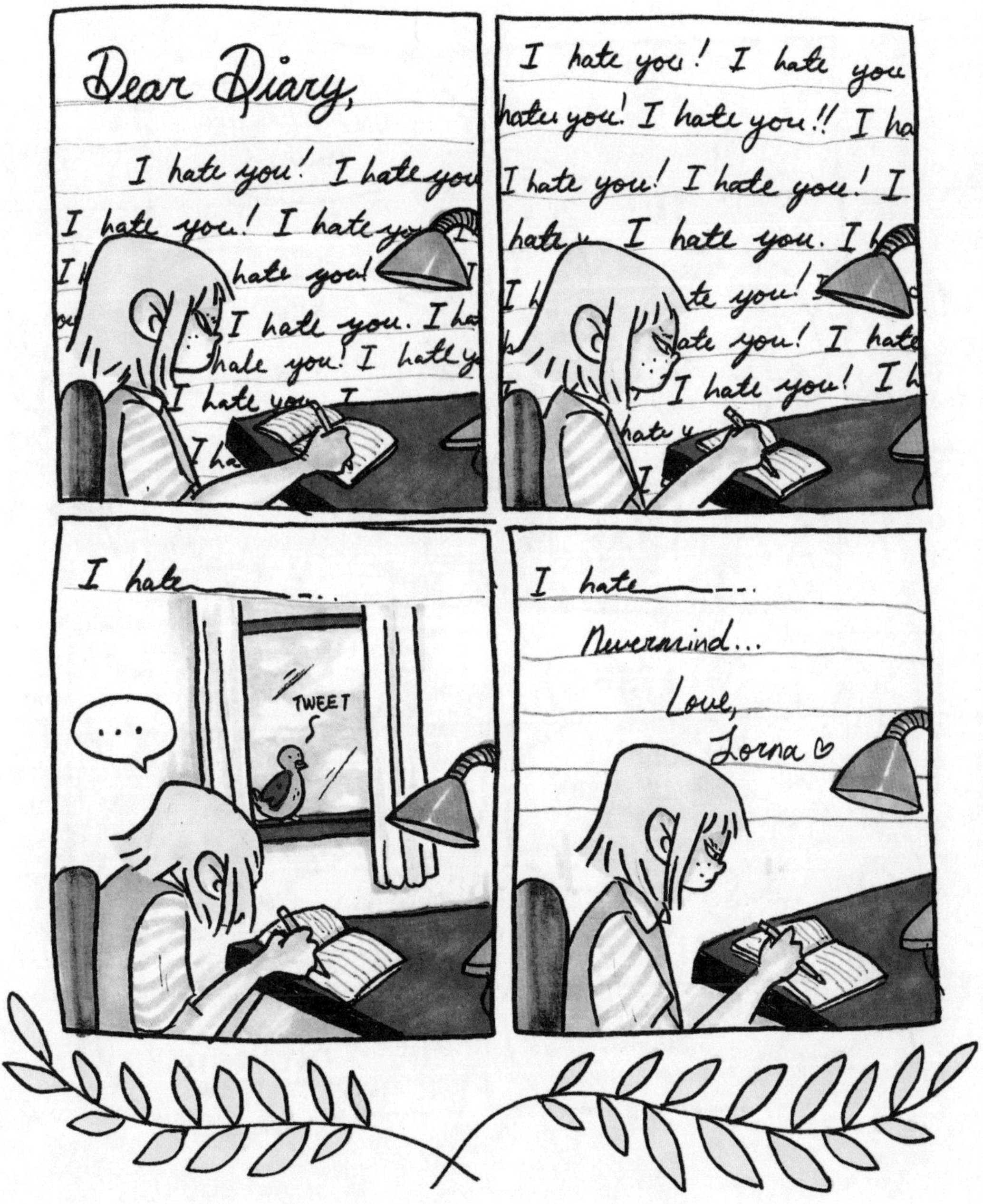
Dear Diary,
I hate you! I hate you
I hate you! I hate you
I hate you. I hate you!
I hate you! I hate you
I hate you!! I ha
I hate you! I hate you! I
I hate you. I
I hate you! I hate
I hate you! I
I hate...
...
TWEET
I hate...
Nevermind...
Love,
Lorna

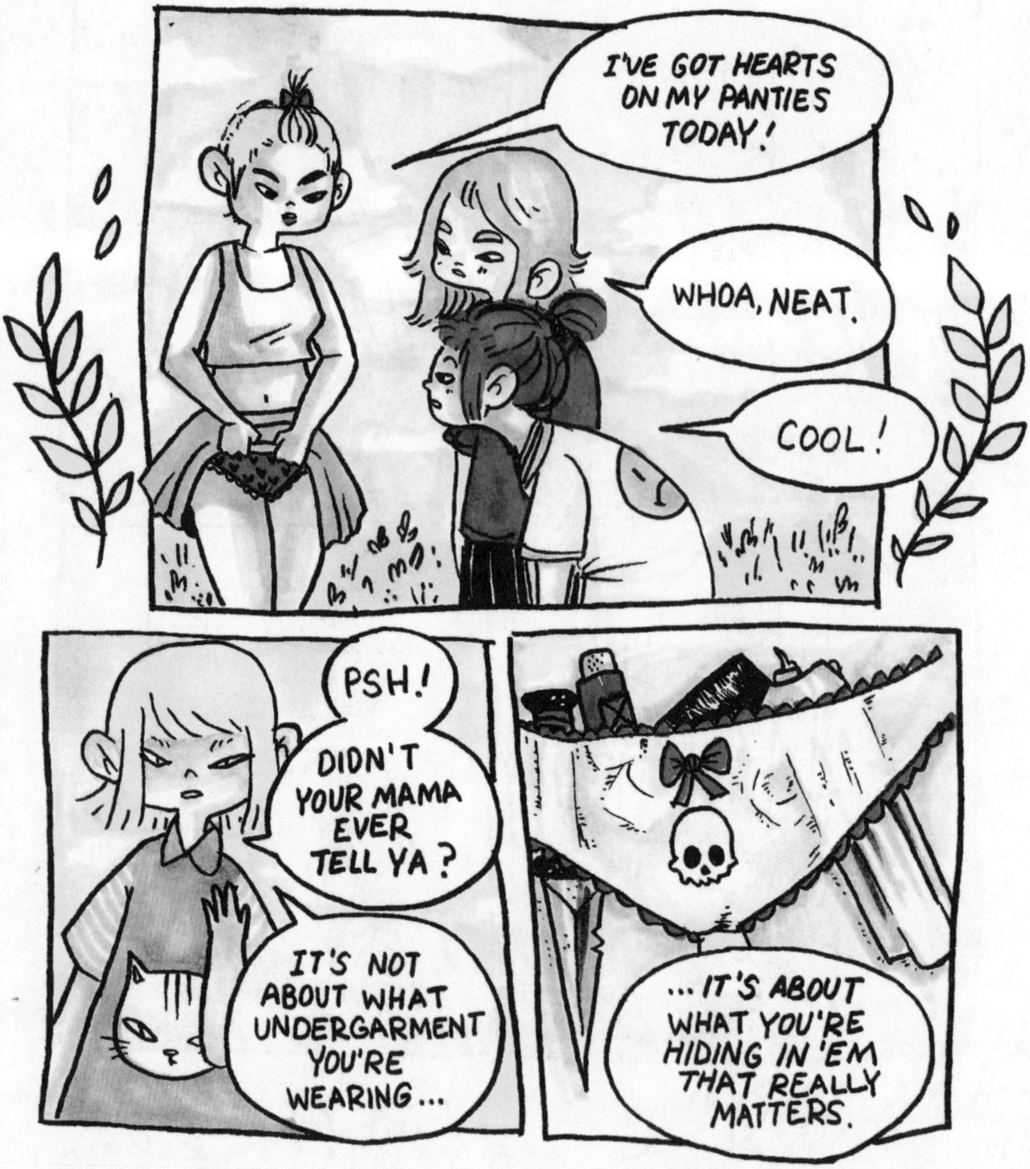
I'VE GOT HEARTS ON MY PANTIES TODAY!
WHOA, NEAT.
COOL!
PSH!
DIDN'T YOUR MAMA EVER TELL YA?
IT'S NOT ABOUT WHAT UNDERGARMENT YOU'RE WEARING...
...IT'S ABOUT WHAT YOU'RE HIDING IN 'EM THAT REALLY MATTERS.

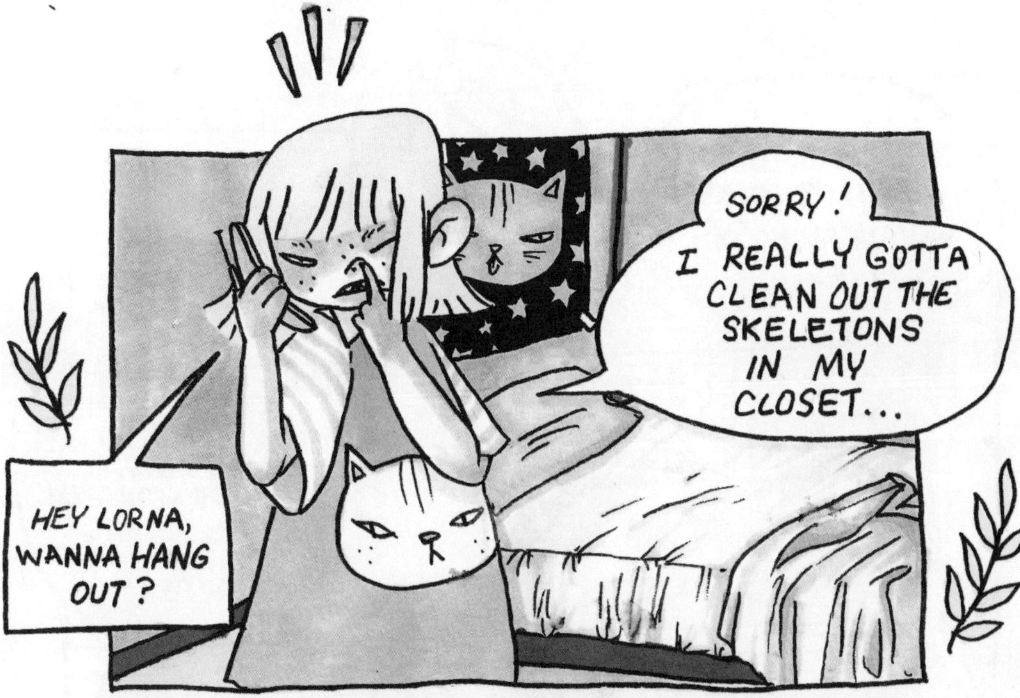
HEY LORNA, WANNA HANG OUT?
SORRY! I REALLY GOTTA CLEAN OUT THE SKELETONS IN MY CLOSET...

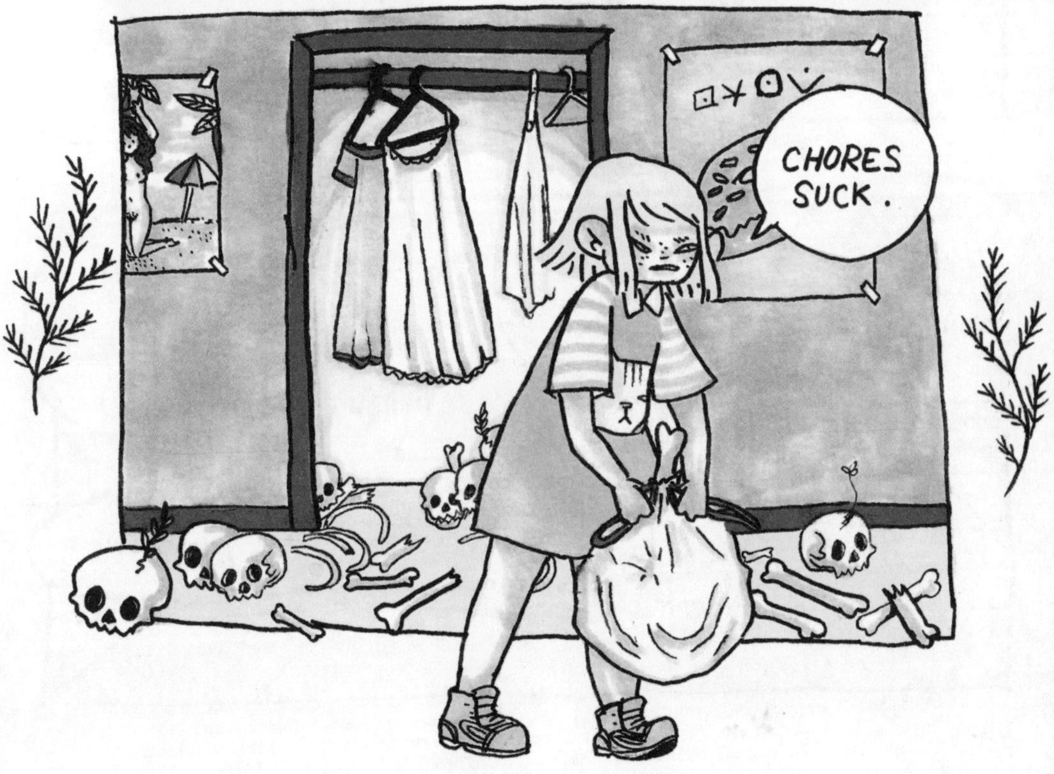
CHORES SUCK.

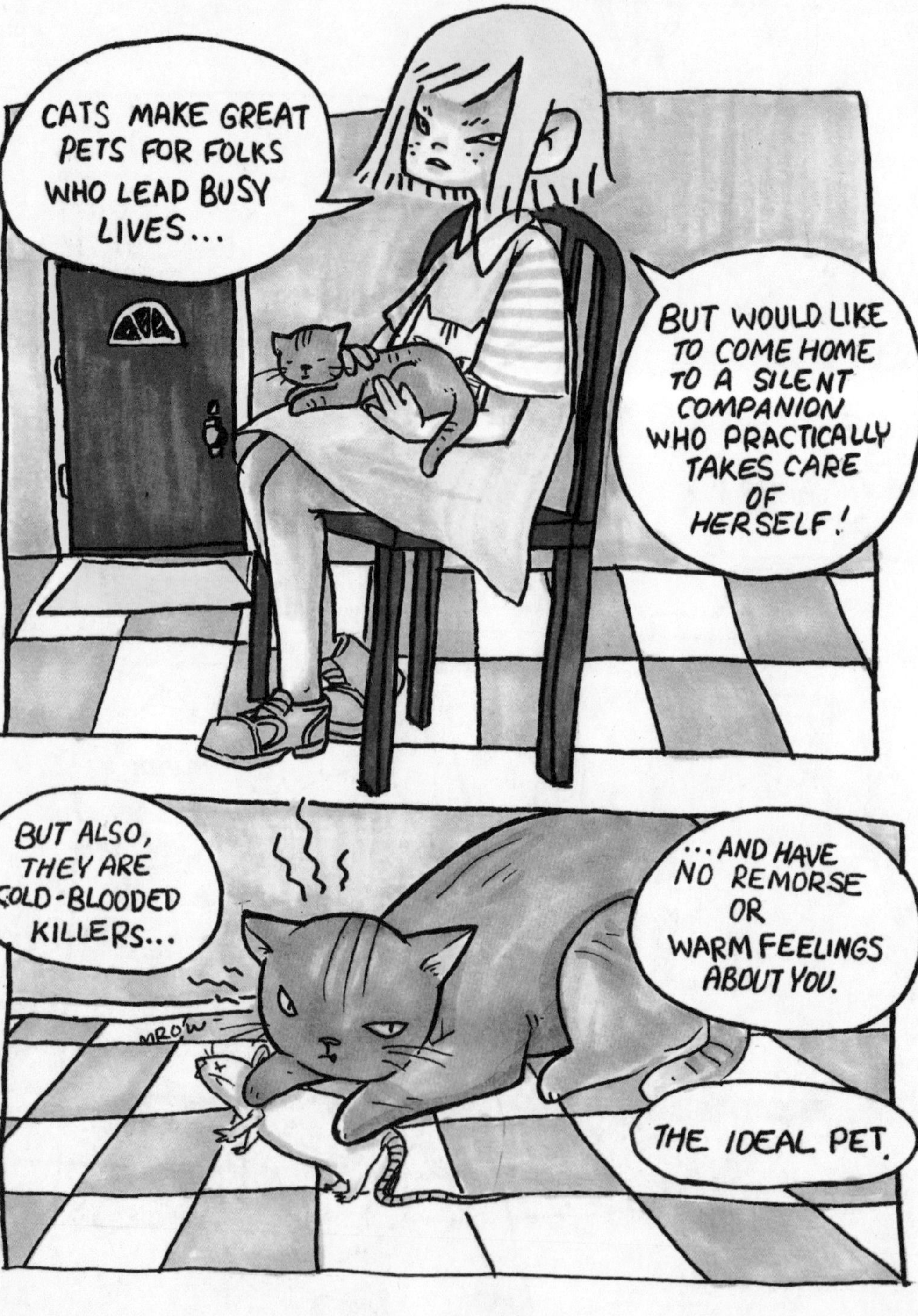
CATS MAKE GREAT PETS FOR FOLKS WHO LEAD BUSY LIVES...
BUT WOULD LIKE TO COME HOME TO A SILENT COMPANION WHO PRACTICALLY TAKES CARE OF HERSELF!
BUT ALSO, THEY ARE COLD-BLOODED KILLERS...
...AND HAVE NO REMORSE OR WARM FEELINGS ABOUT YOU.
MROW
THE IDEAL PET.

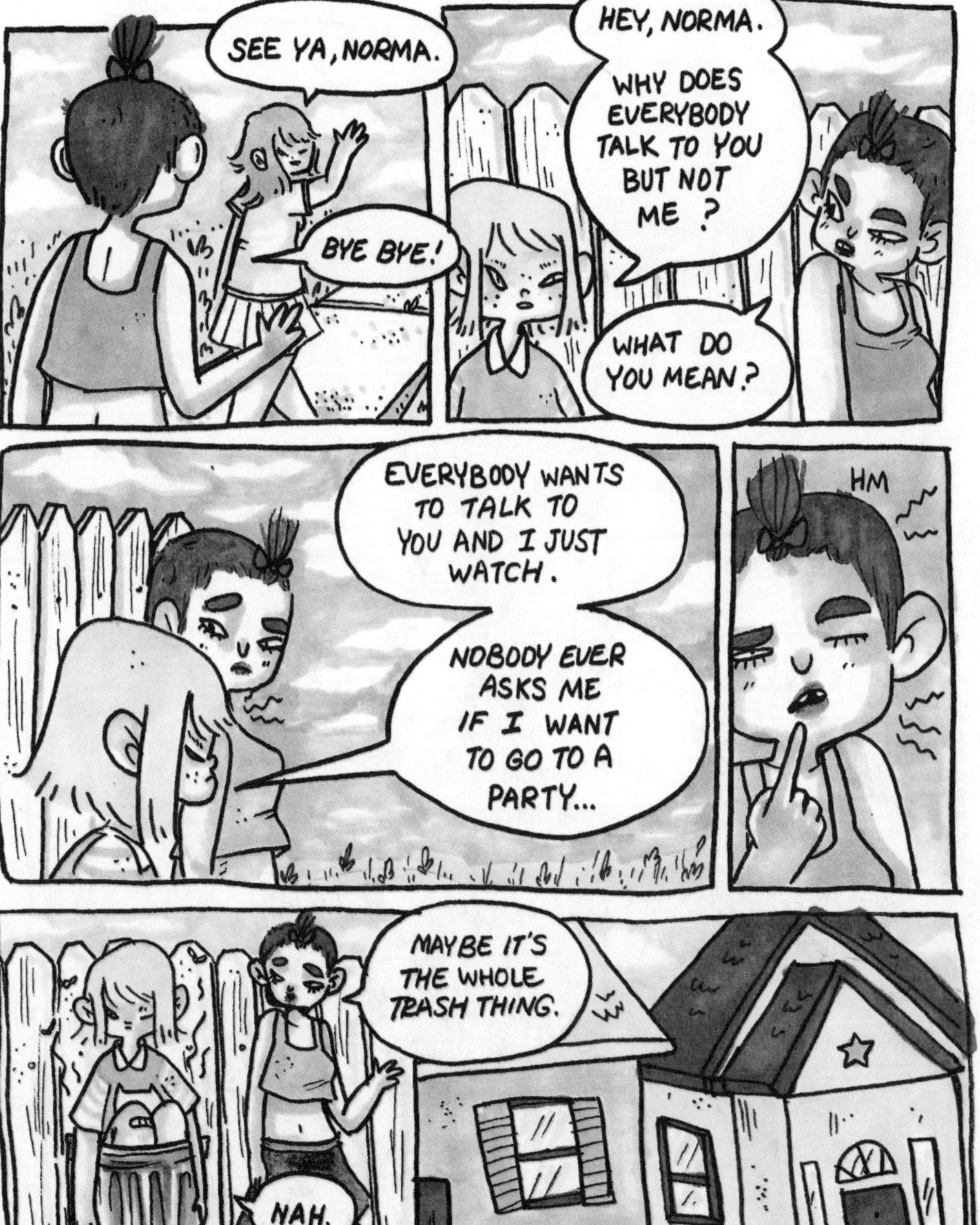

SEE YA, NORMA.
BYE BYE!
HEY, NORMA.
WHY DOES EVERYBODY TALK TO YOU BUT NOT ME ?
WHAT DO YOU MEAN?
EVERYBODY WANTS TO TALK TO YOU AND I JUST WATCH.
NOBODY EVER ASKS ME IF I WANT TO GO TO A PARTY...
HM
MAYBE IT'S THE WHOLE TRASH THING.
NAH.

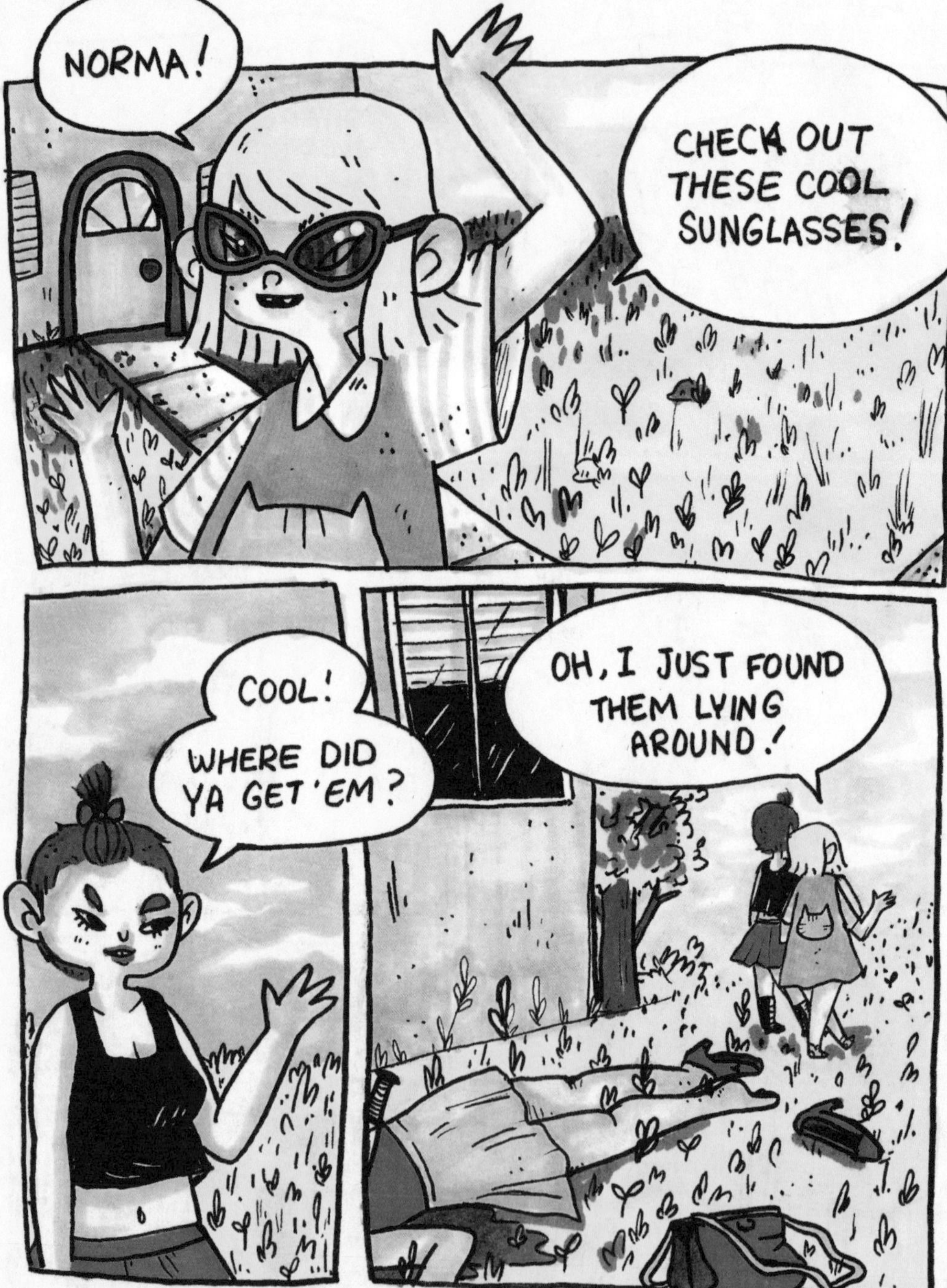
NORMA!
CHECK OUT THESE COOL SUNGLASSES!
COOL!
WHERE DID YA GET 'EM?
OH, I JUST FOUND THEM LYING AROUND!

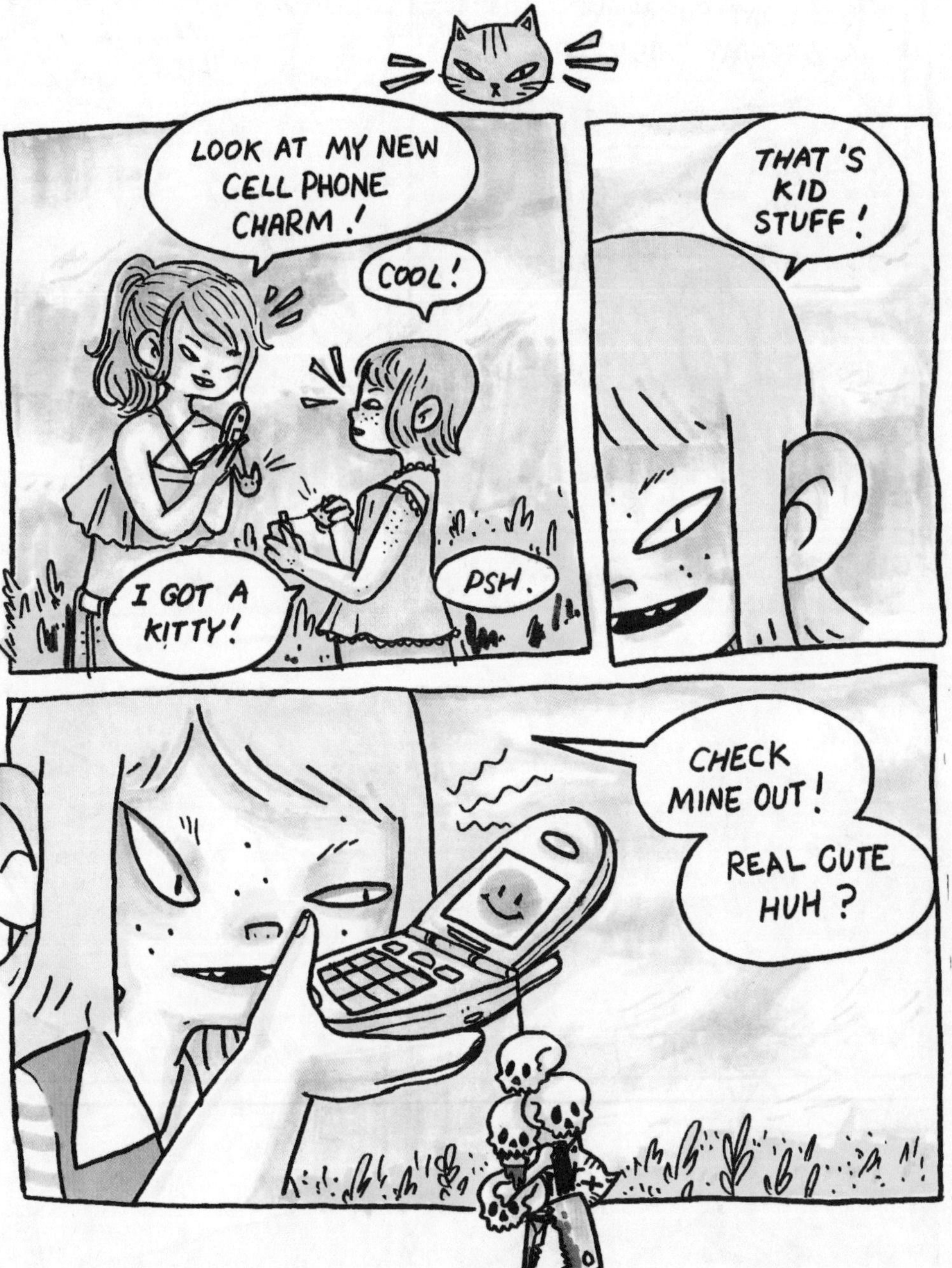
LOOK AT MY NEW CELL PHONE CHARM!
COOL!
I GOT A KITTY!
PSH.
THAT'S KID STUFF!
CHECK MINE OUT!
REAL CUTE HUH?

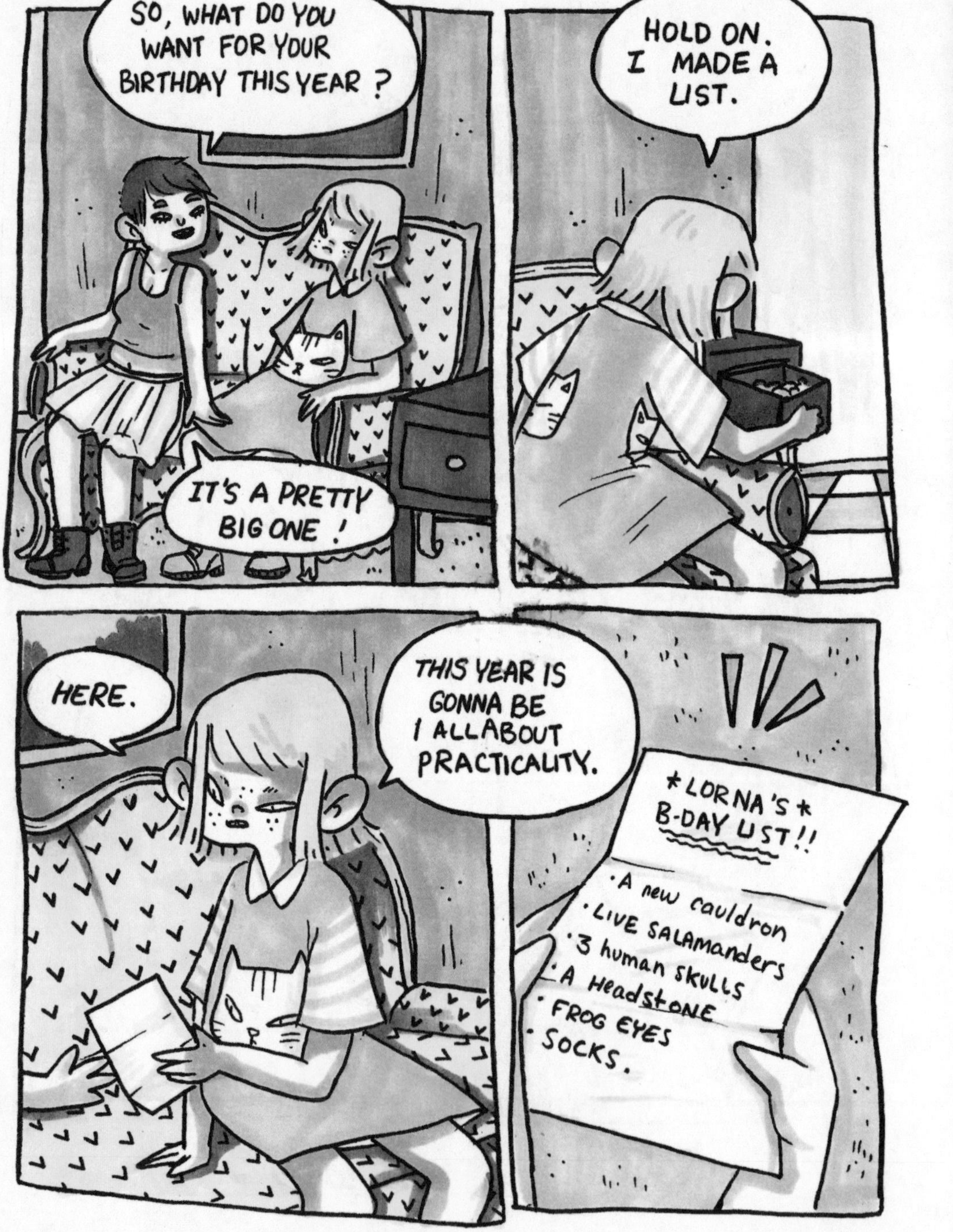
SO, WHAT DO YOU WANT FOR YOUR BIRTHDAY THIS YEAR ?
IT'S A PRETTY BIG ONE !
HOLD ON. I MADE A LIST.
HERE.
THIS YEAR IS GONNA BE I ALLABOUT PRACTICALITY.
LORNA'S B-DAY LIST!!
·A new cauldron
·LIVE SALAMANDERS
·3 human SKULLS
·A Headstone
·FROG EYES
·SOCKS.

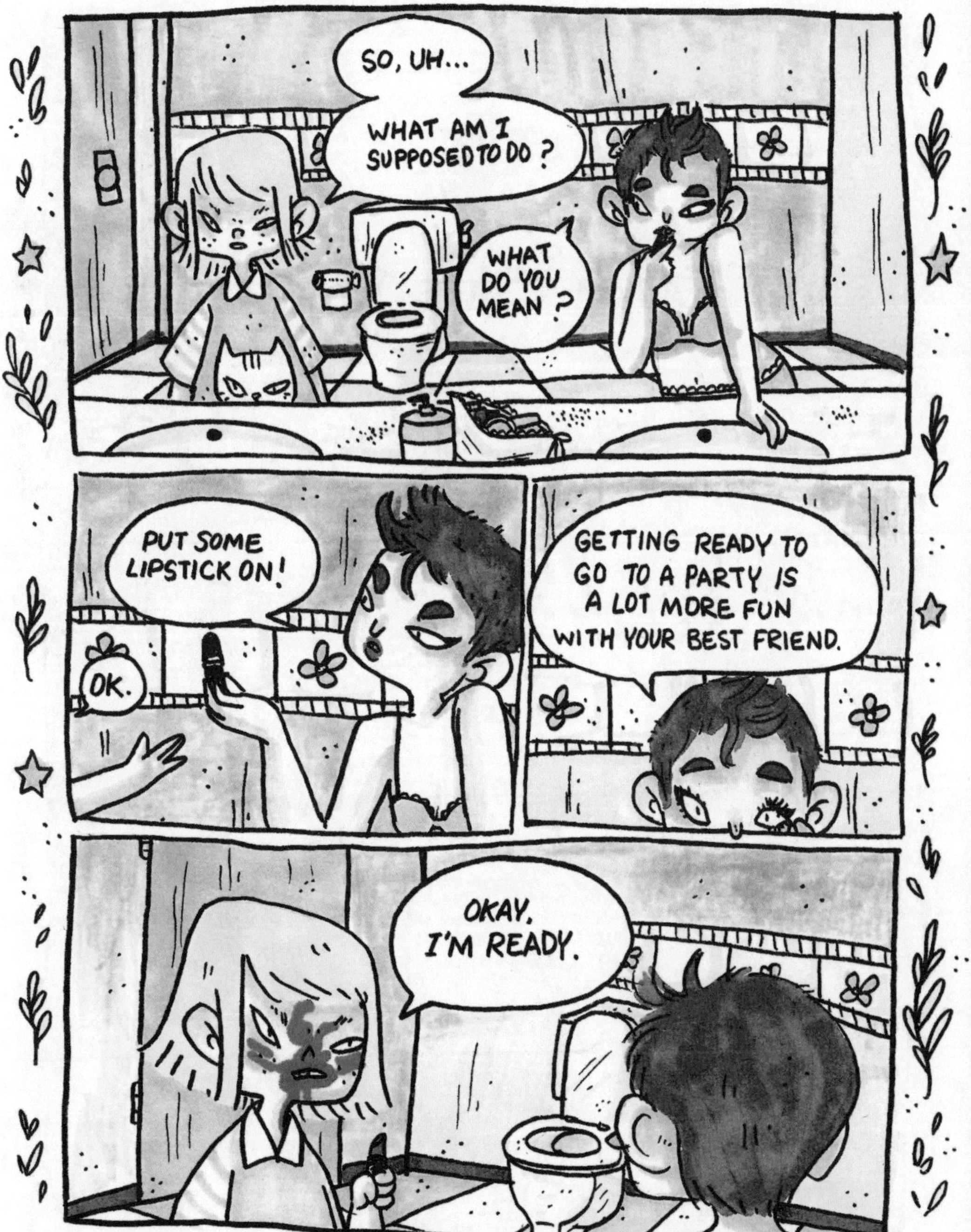
SO, UH...
WHAT AM I SUPPOSED TO DO?
WHAT DO YOU MEAN?
PUT SOME LIPSTICK ON!
OK.
GETTING READY TO GO TO A PARTY IS A LOT MORE FUN WITH YOUR BEST FRIEND.
OKAY, I'M READY.

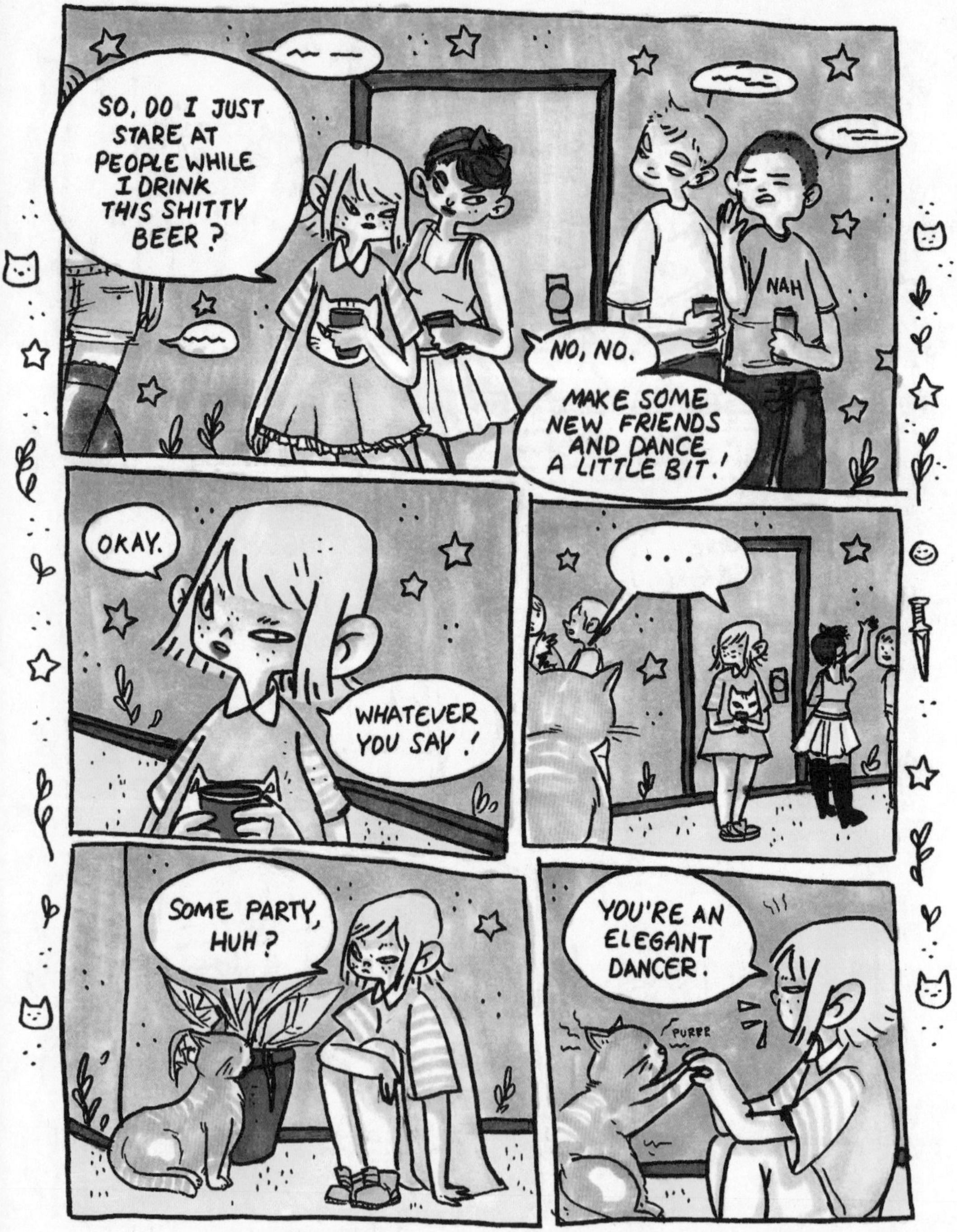

SO, DO I JUST STARE AT PEOPLE WHILE I DRINK THIS SHITTY BEER?
NAH
NO, NO.
MAKE SOME NEW FRIENDS AND DANCE A LITTLE BIT!
OKAY.
WHATEVER YOU SAY!
...
SOME PARTY, HUH?
YOU'RE AN ELEGANT DANCER.
PURRR

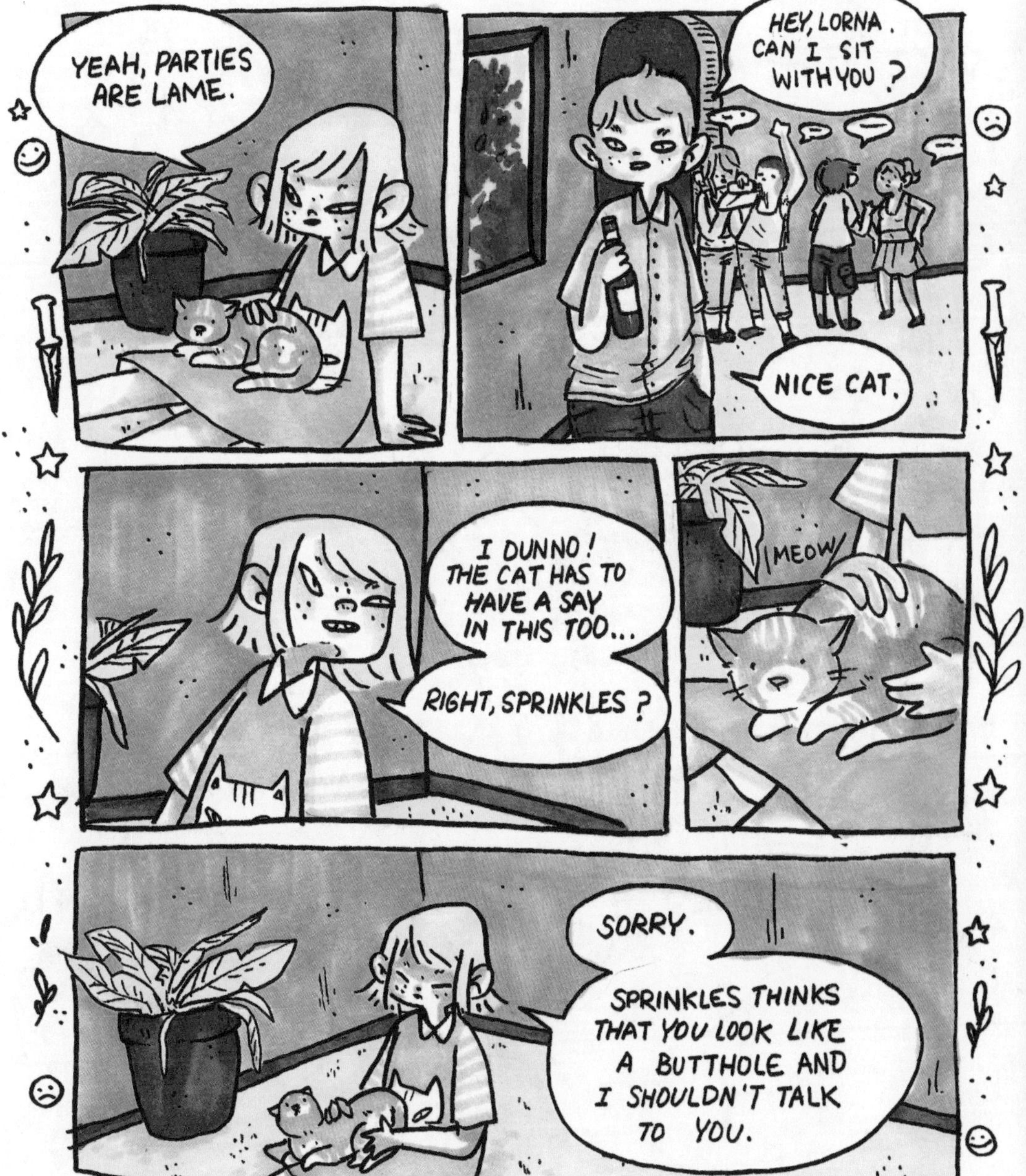
YEAH, PARTIES ARE LAME.
HEY, LORNA. CAN I SIT WITH YOU ?
NICE CAT.
I DUNNO! THE CAT HAS TO HAVE A SAY IN THIS TOO...
RIGHT, SPRINKLES ?
MEOW
SORRY.
SPRINKLES THINKS THAT YOU LOOK LIKE A BUTTHOLE AND I SHOULDN'T TALK TO YOU.

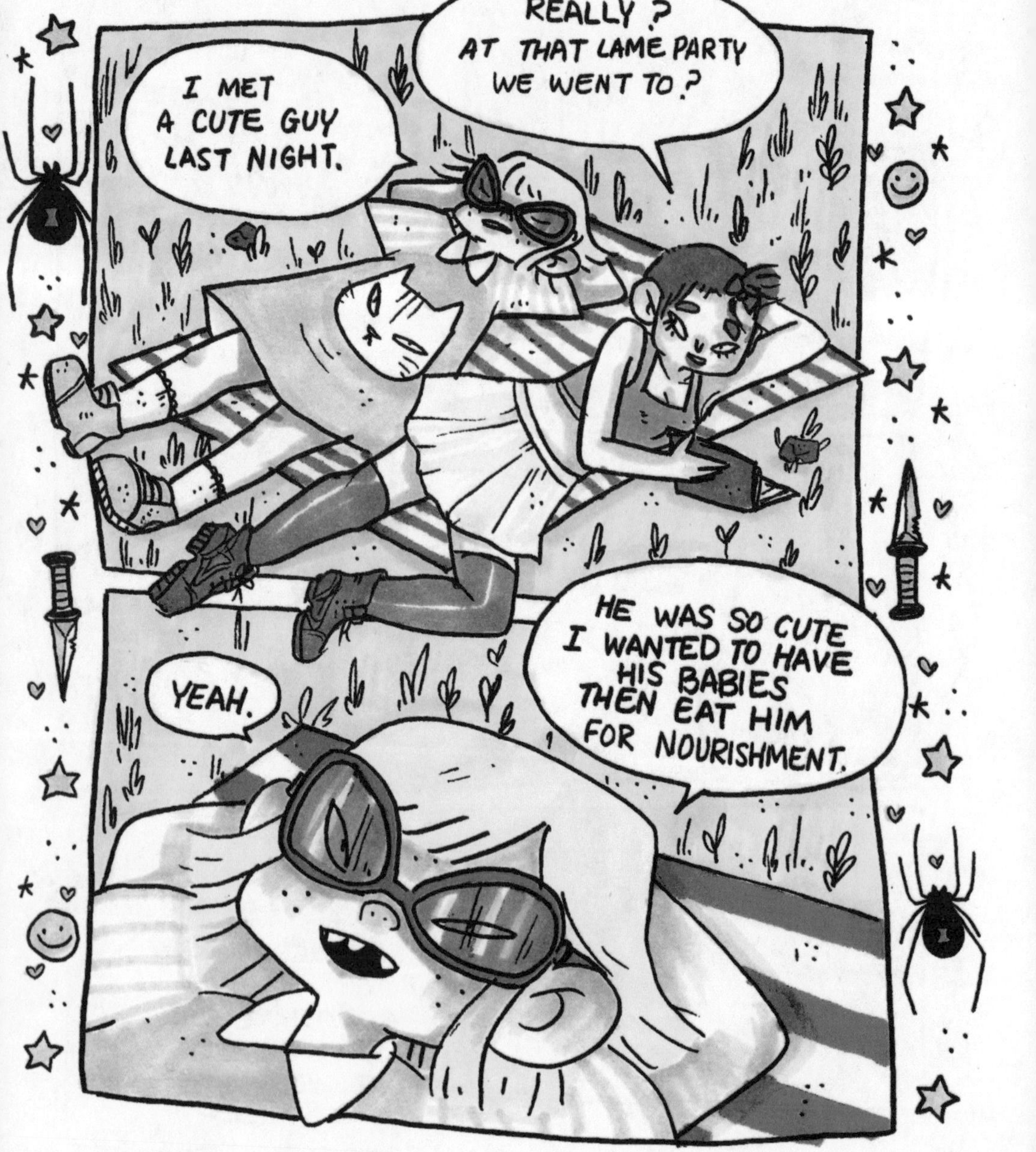
I MET A CUTE GUY LAST NIGHT.
REALLY ? AT THAT LAME PARTY WE WENT TO ?
YEAH.
HE WAS SO CUTE I WANTED TO HAVE HIS BABIES THEN EAT HIM FOR NOURISHMENT.

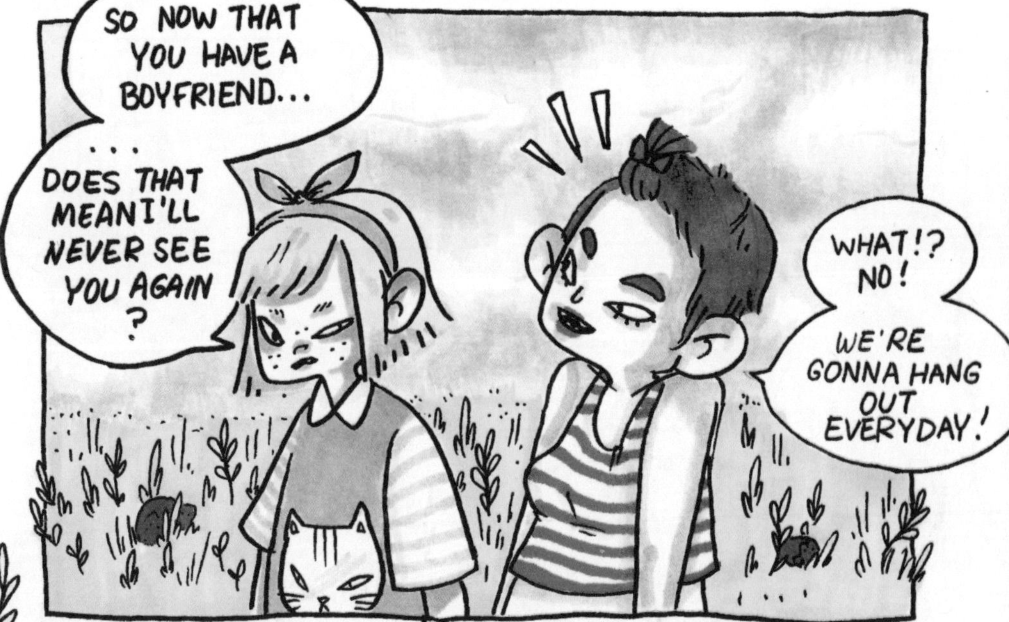
SO NOW THAT YOU HAVE A BOYFRIEND...
... DOES THAT MEAN I'LL NEVER SEE YOU AGAIN ?
WHAT!? NO!
WE'RE GONNA HANG OUT EVERYDAY!

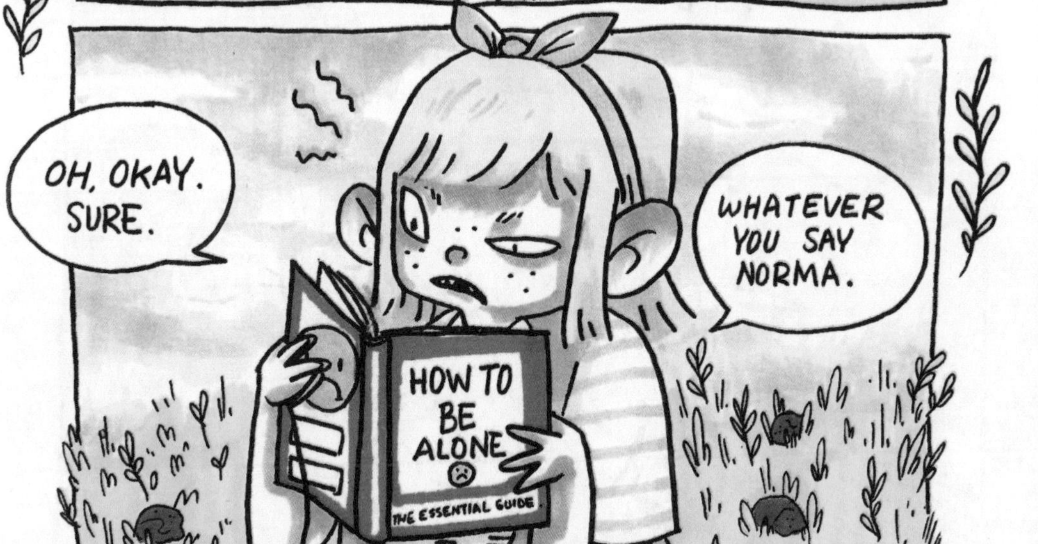
OH, OKAY. SURE.
HOW TO BE ALONE
THE ESSENTIAL GUIDE
WHATEVER YOU SAY NORMA.

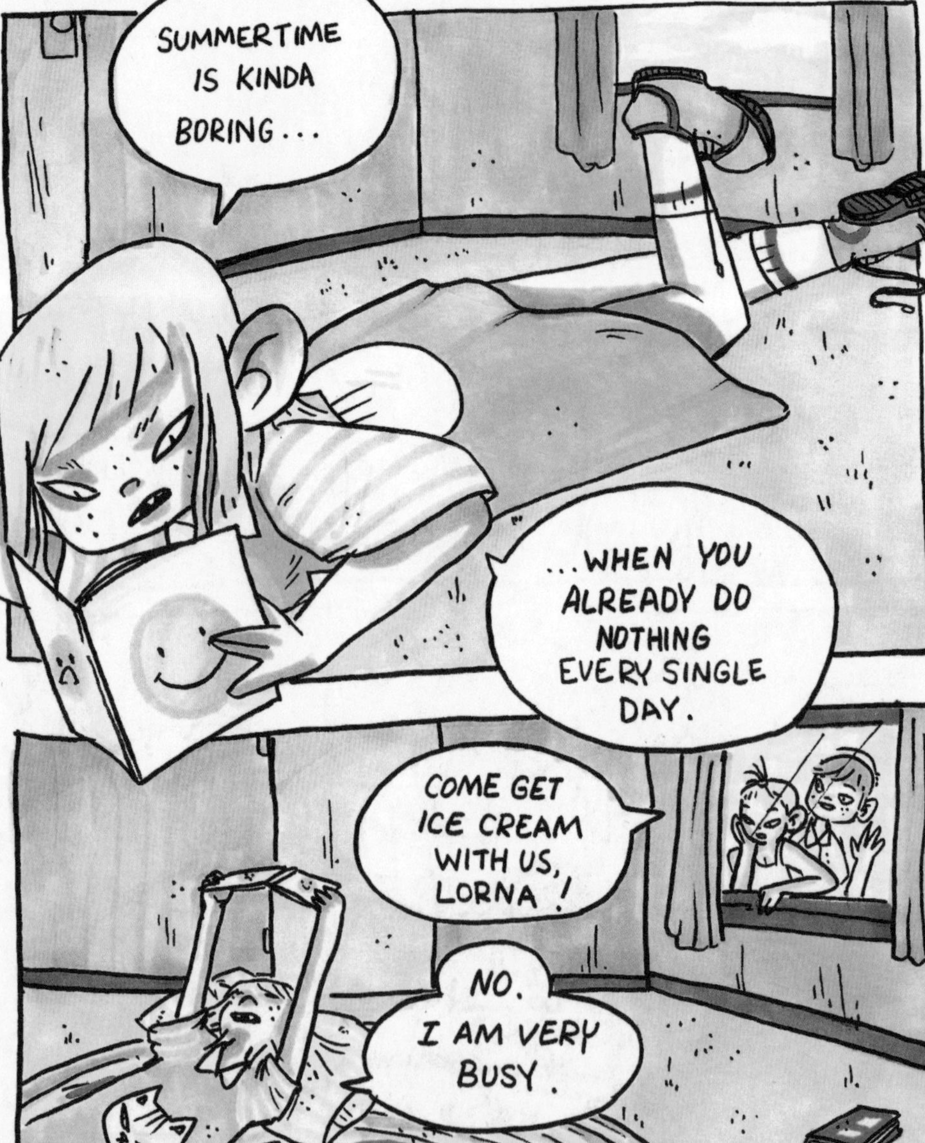
SUMMERTIME IS KINDA BORING...
...WHEN YOU ALREADY DO NOTHING EVERY SINGLE DAY.
COME GET ICE CREAM WITH US, LORNA!
NO. I AM VERY BUSY.

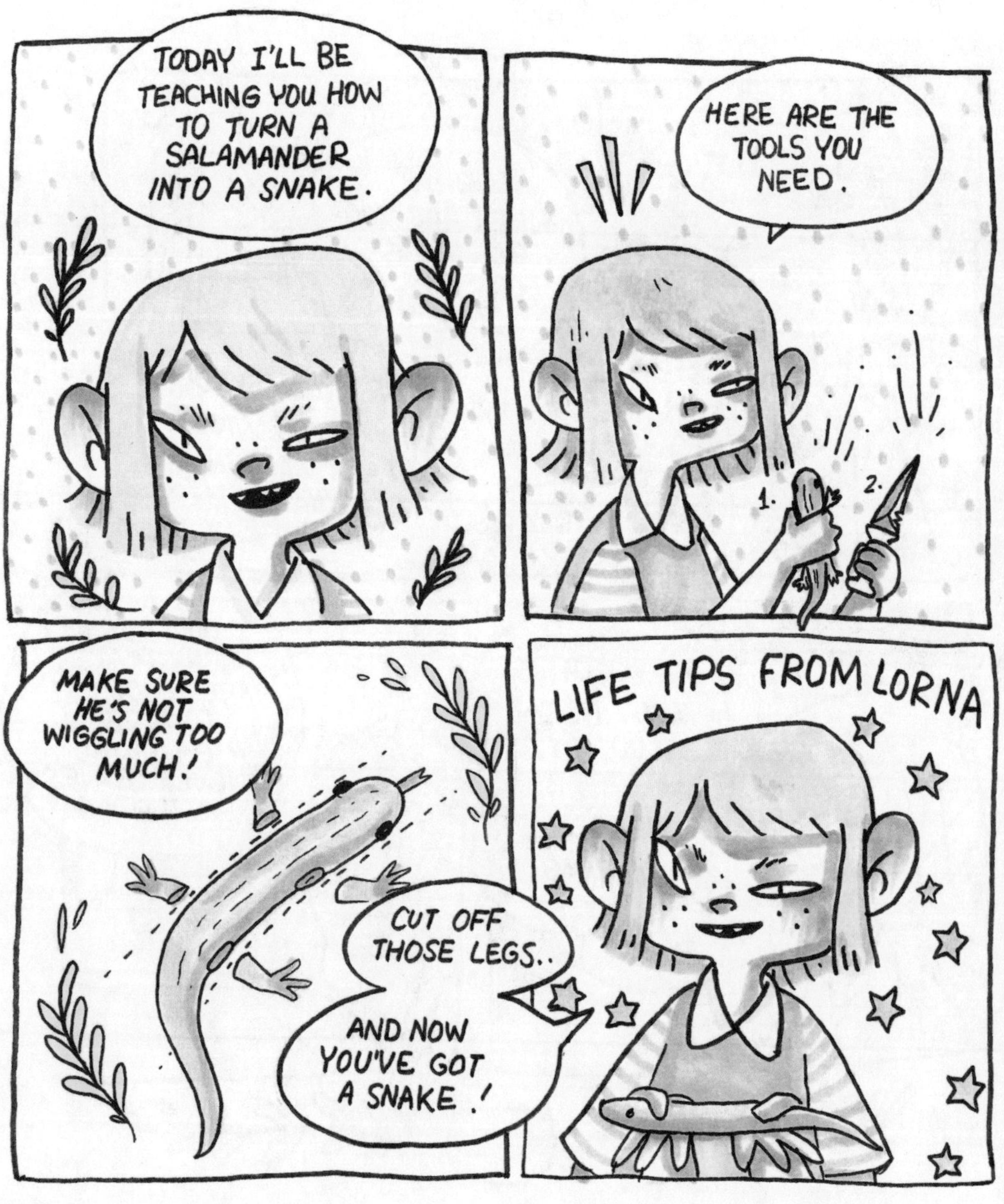
TODAY I'LL BE TEACHING YOU HOW TO TURN A SALAMANDER INTO A SNAKE.
HERE ARE THE TOOLS YOU NEED.
1.
2.
MAKE SURE HE'S NOT WIGGLING TOO MUCH!
CUT OFF THOSE LEGS..
AND NOW YOU'VE GOT A SNAKE!
LIFE TIPS FROM LORNA

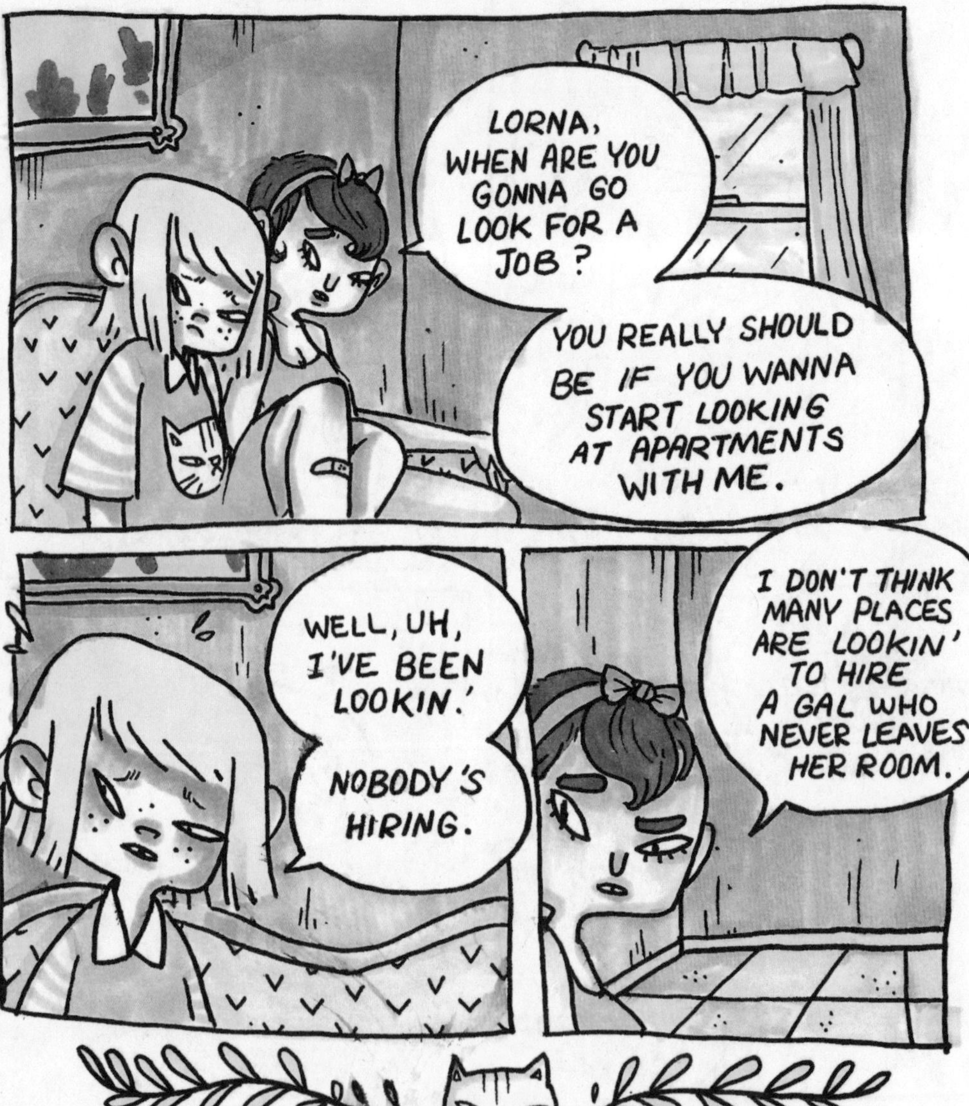
LORNA, WHEN ARE YOU GONNA GO LOOK FOR A JOB?
YOU REALLY SHOULD BE IF YOU WANNA START LOOKING AT APARTMENTS WITH ME.
WELL, UH, I'VE BEEN LOOKIN.'
NOBODY'S HIRING.
I DON'T THINK MANY PLACES ARE LOOKIN' TO HIRE A GAL WHO NEVER LEAVES HER ROOM.

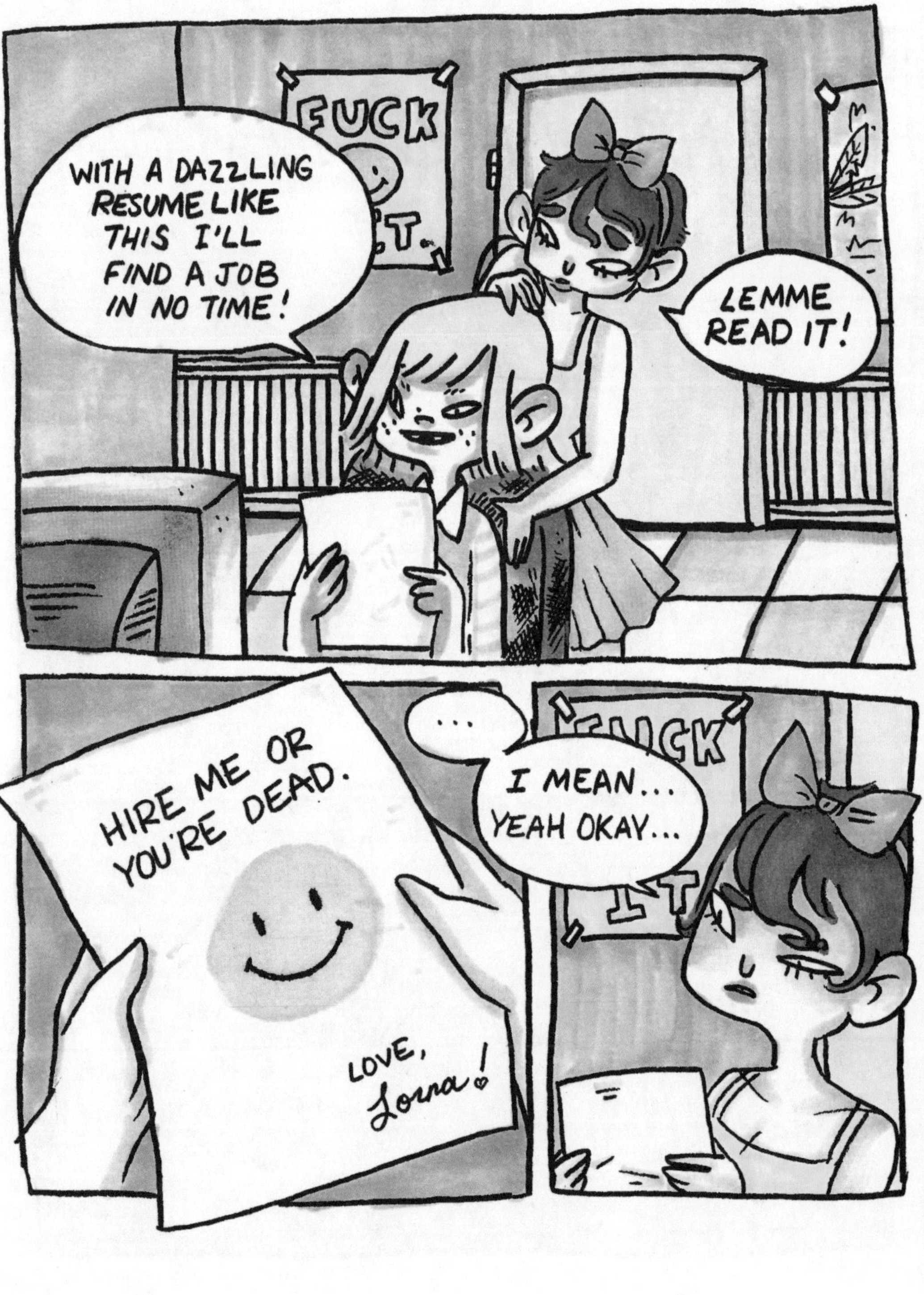
FUCK
WITH A DAZZLING RESUME LIKE THIS I'LL FIND A JOB IN NO TIME!
LEMME READ IT!
HIRE ME OR YOU'RE DEAD.
LOVE, Lorna!
...
I MEAN... YEAH OKAY...

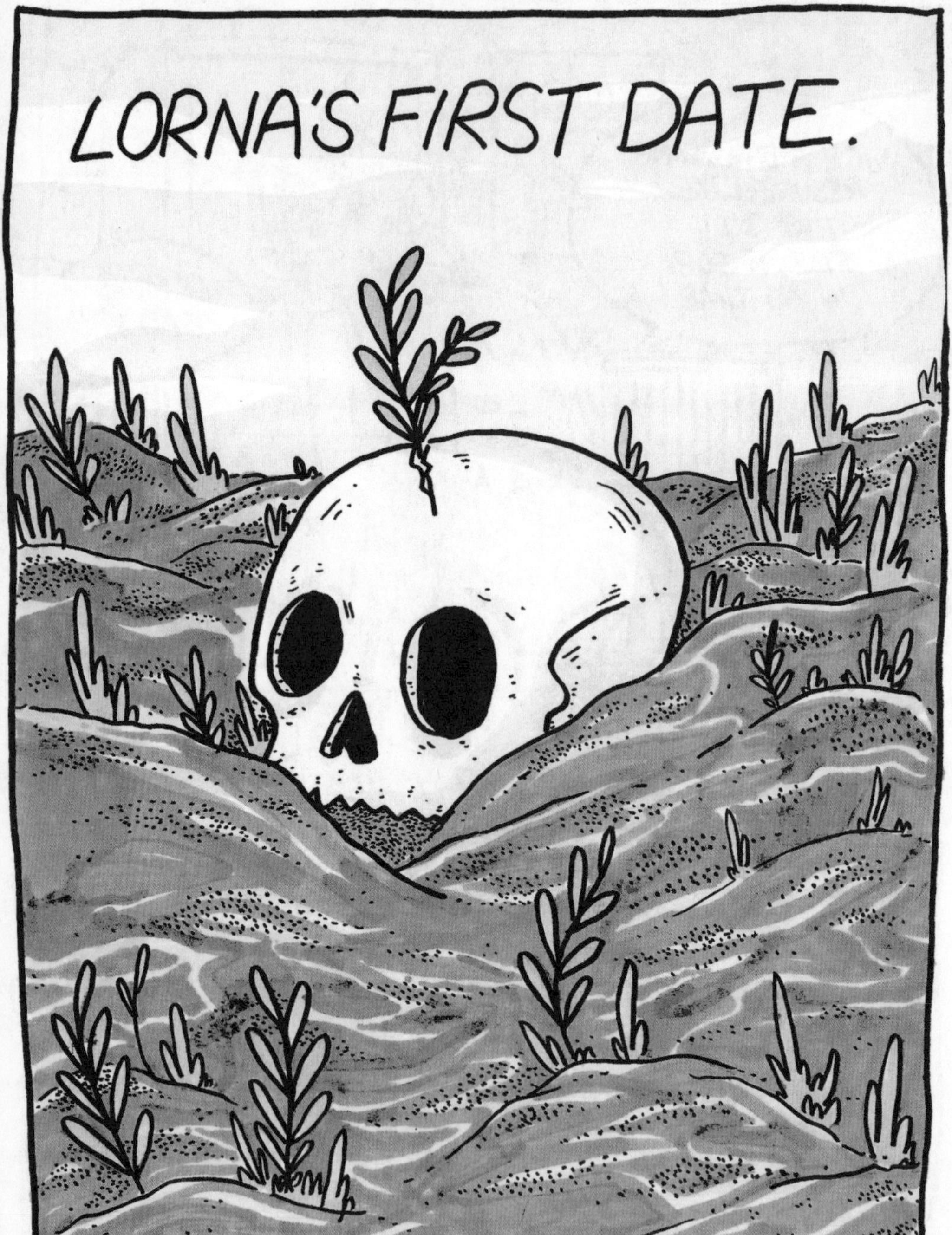
LORNA'S FIRST DATE.

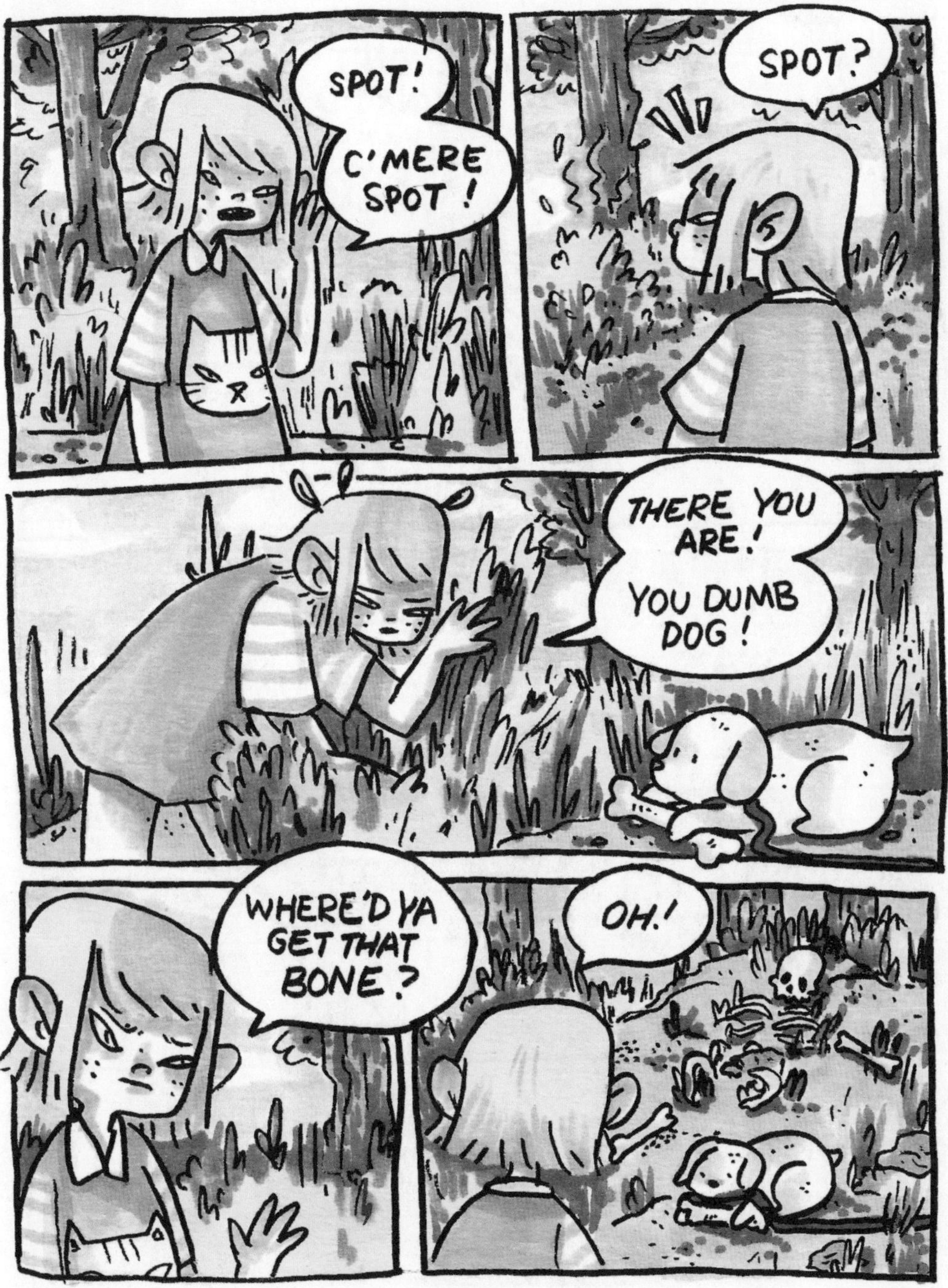
SPOT!
C'MERE SPOT!
SPOT?
THERE YOU ARE!
YOU DUMB DOG!
WHERE'D YA GET THAT BONE?
OH!

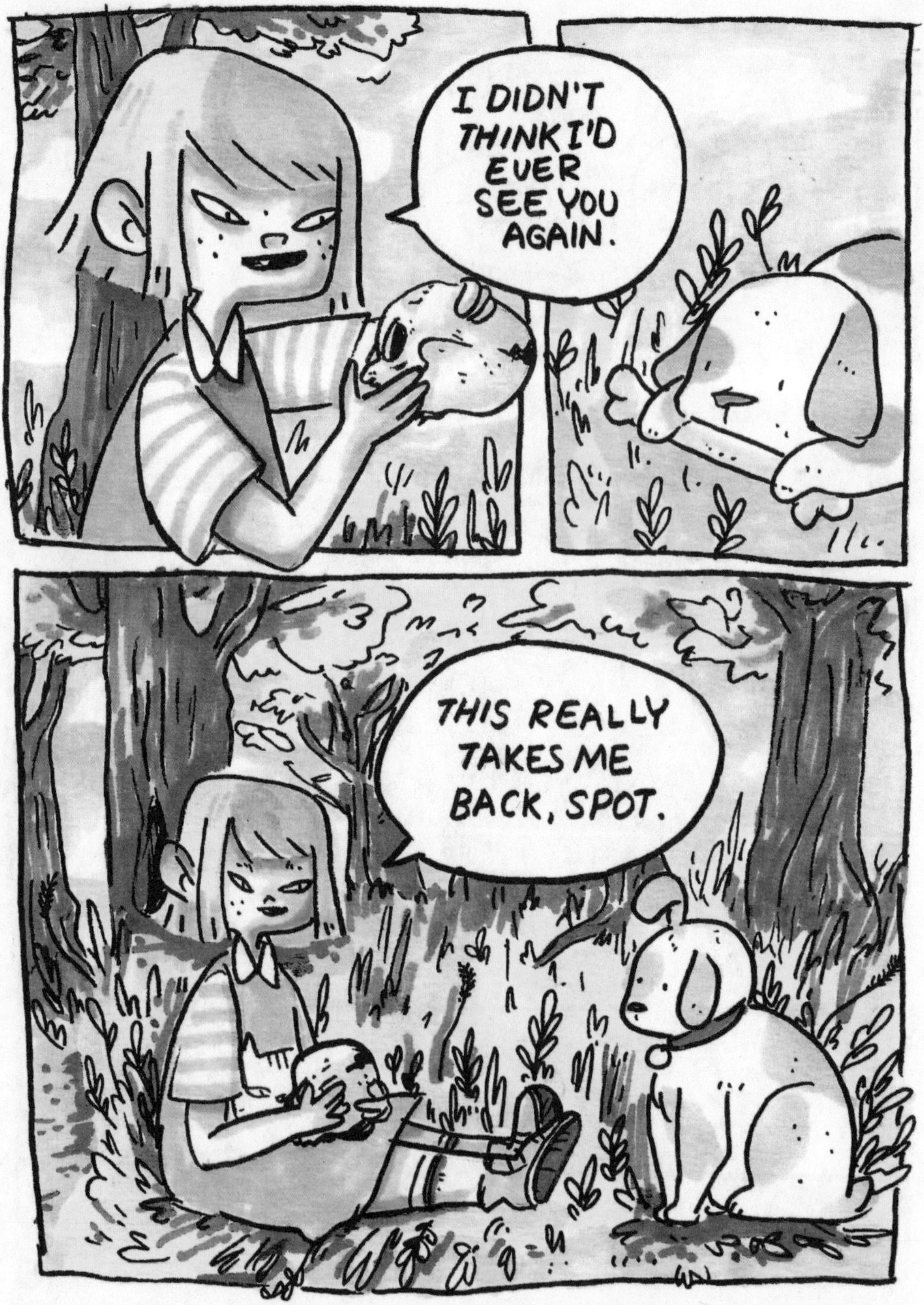
I DIDN'T THINK I'D EVER SEE YOU AGAIN.
THIS REALLY TAKES ME BACK, SPOT.

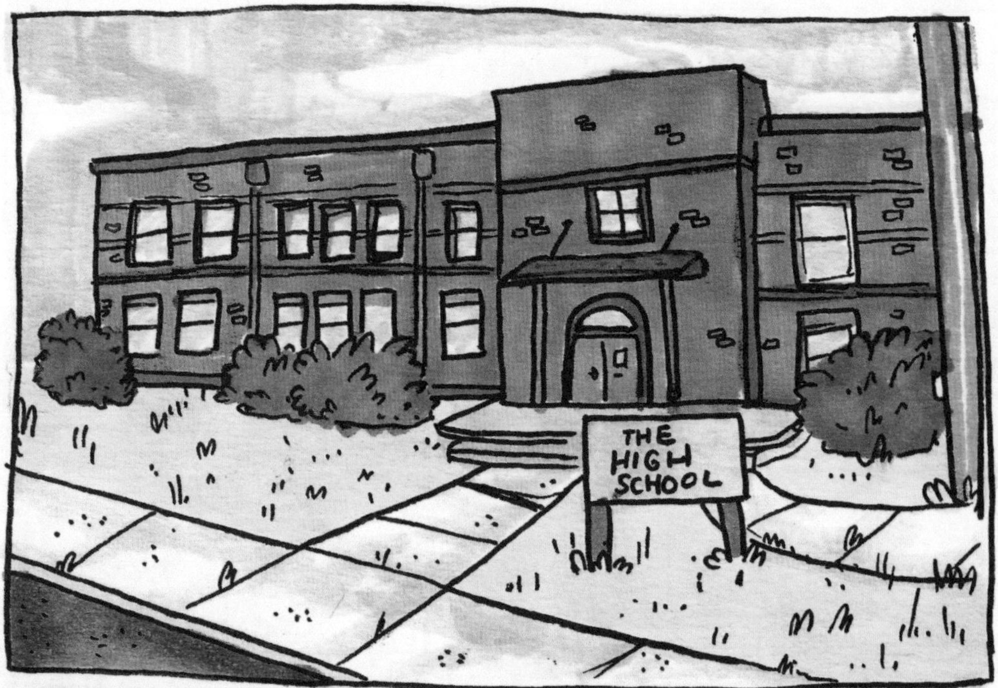
THE HIGH SCHOOL

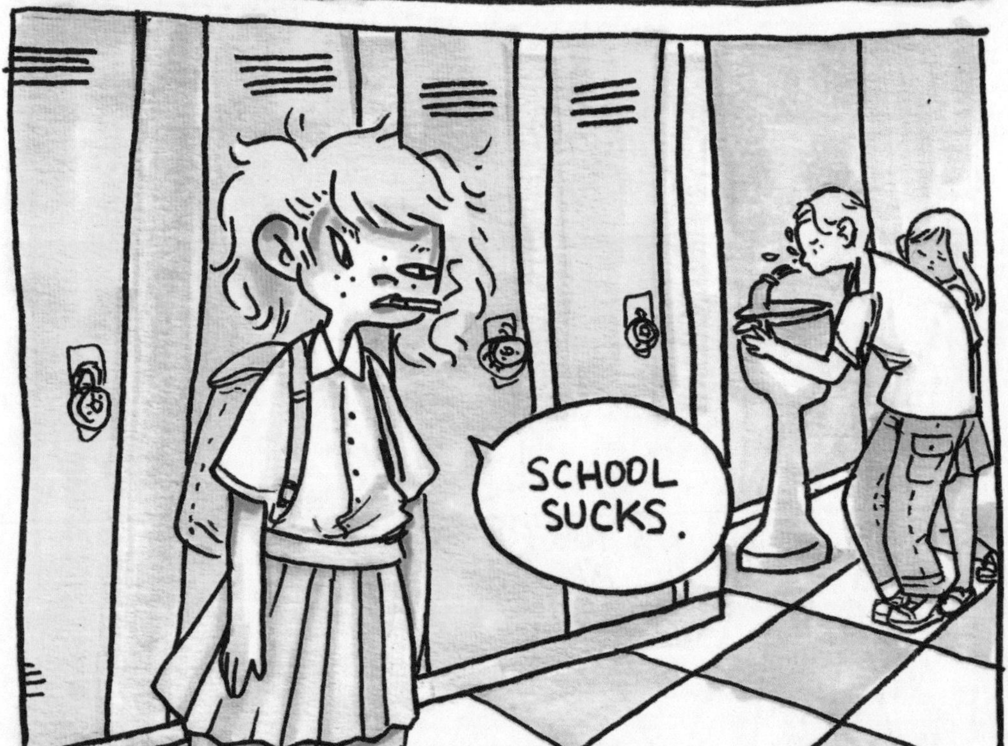
SCHOOL SUCKS.

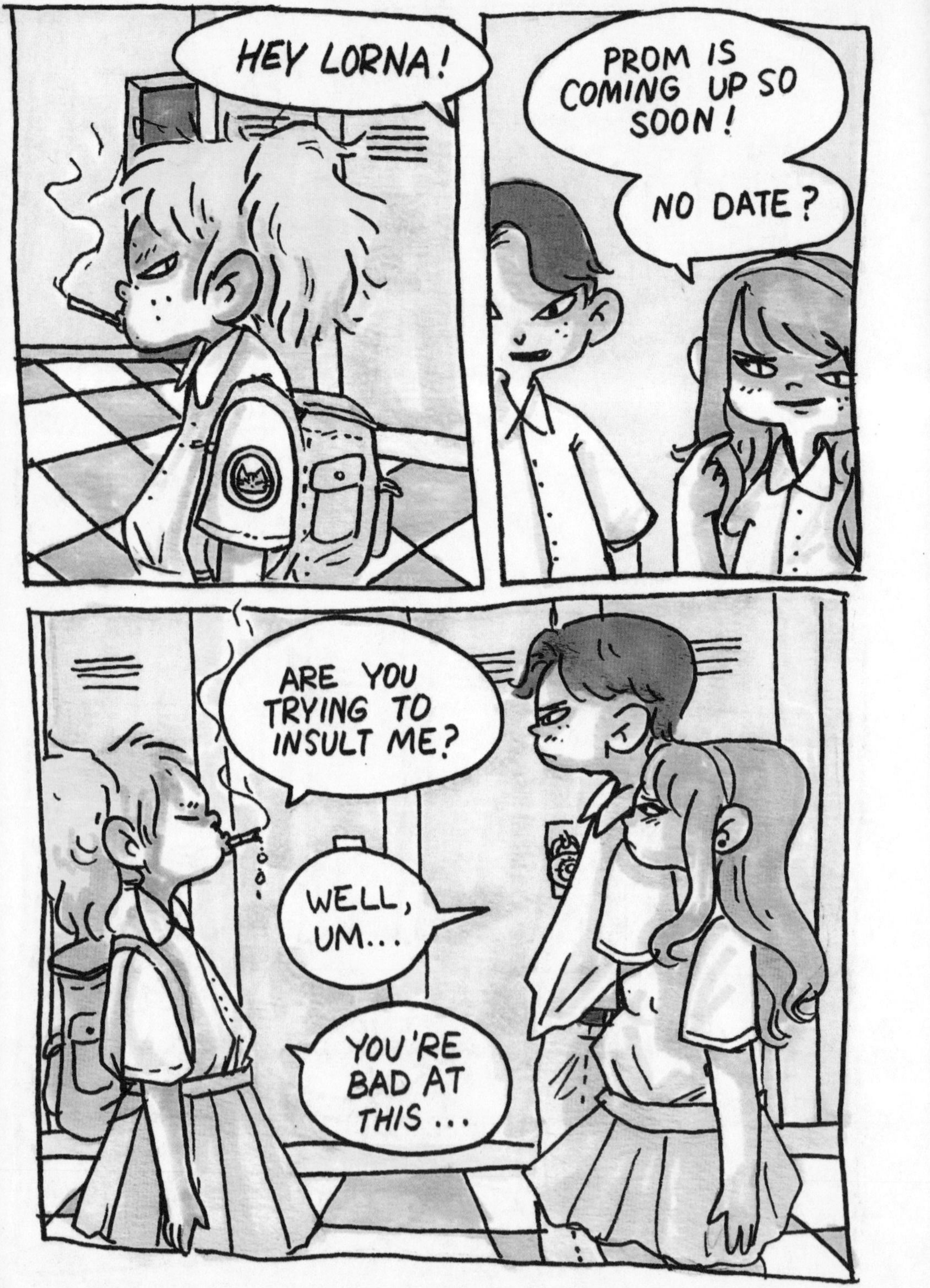
HEY LORNA!
PROM IS COMING UP SO SOON!
NO DATE?
ARE YOU TRYING TO INSULT ME?
WELL, UM...
YOU'RE BAD AT THIS ...

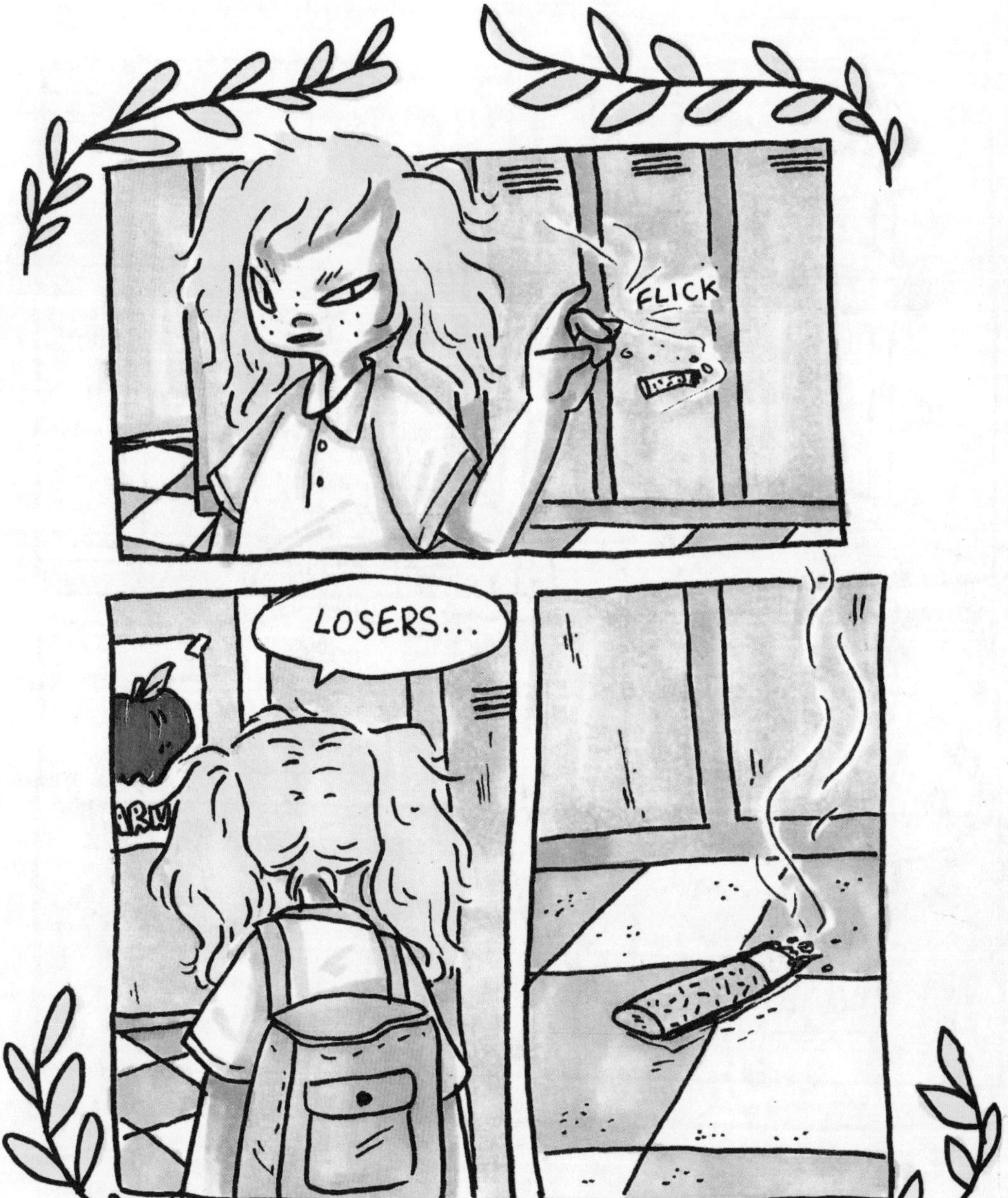
FLICK
LOSERS...

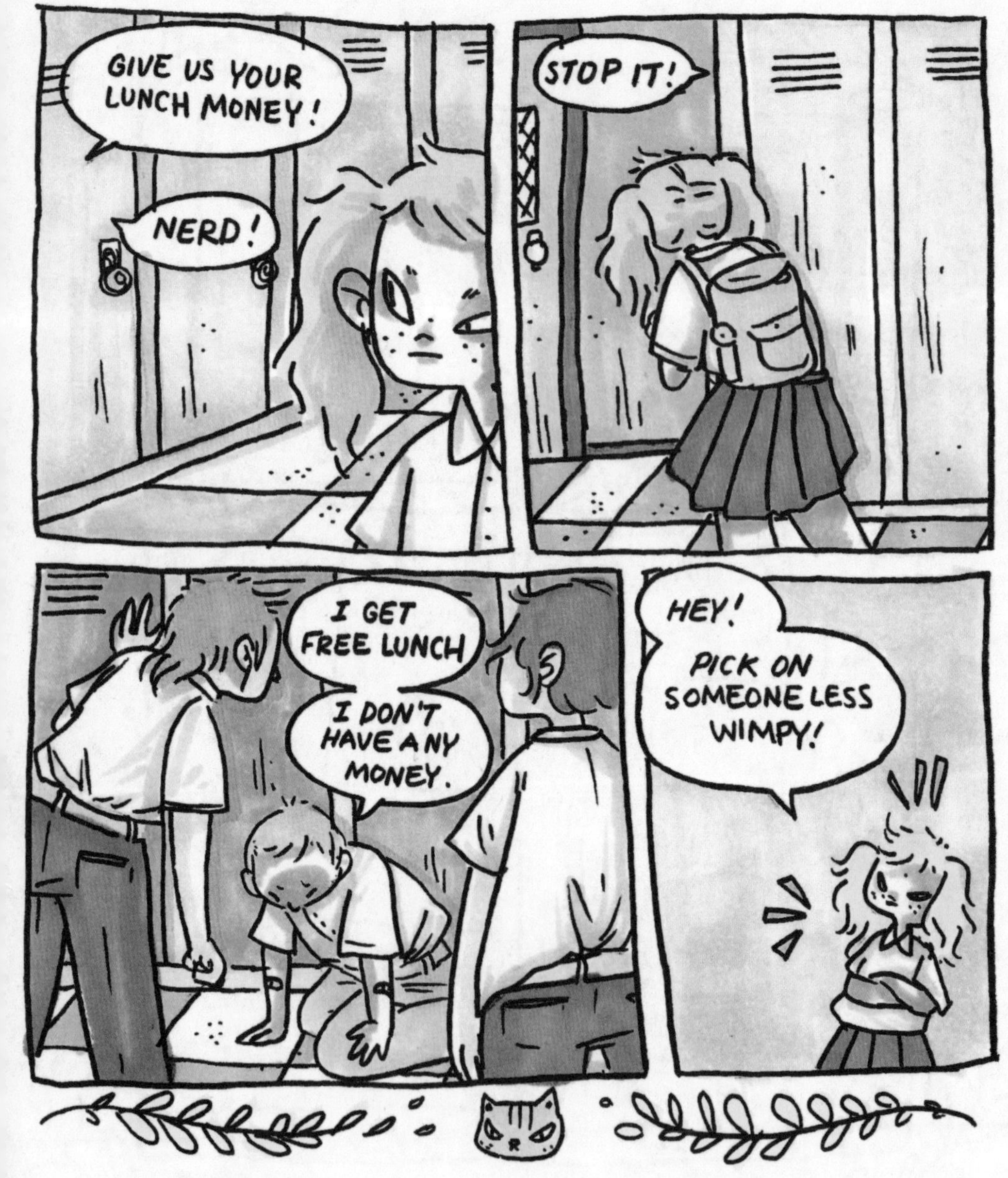
GIVE US YOUR LUNCH MONEY!
NERD!
STOP IT!
I GET FREE LUNCH
I DON'T HAVE ANY MONEY.
HEY!
PICK ON SOMEONE LESS WIMPY!

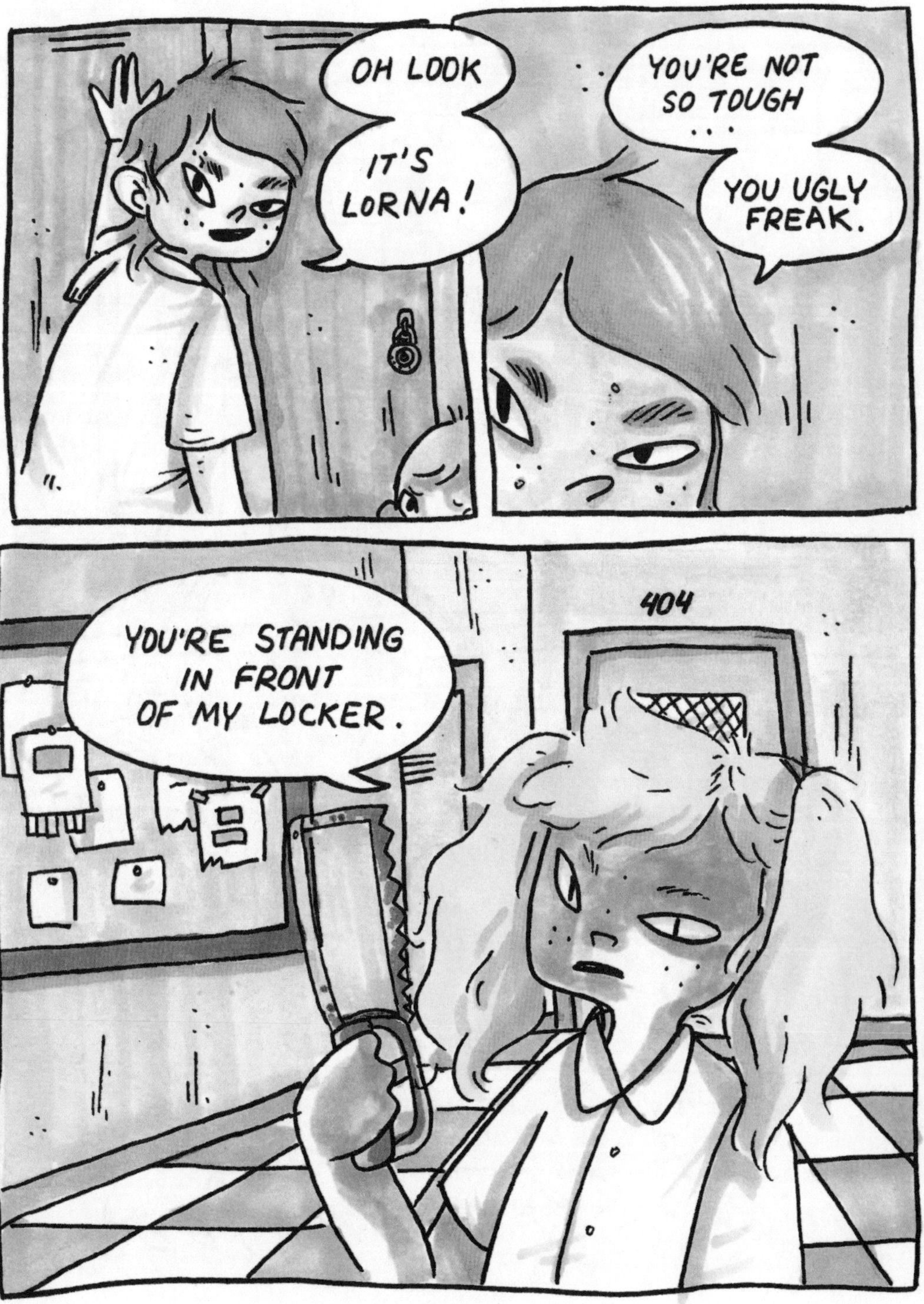
OH LOOK
IT'S LORNA!
YOU'RE NOT SO TOUGH . . .
YOU UGLY FREAK.
YOU'RE STANDING IN FRONT OF MY LOCKER.
404

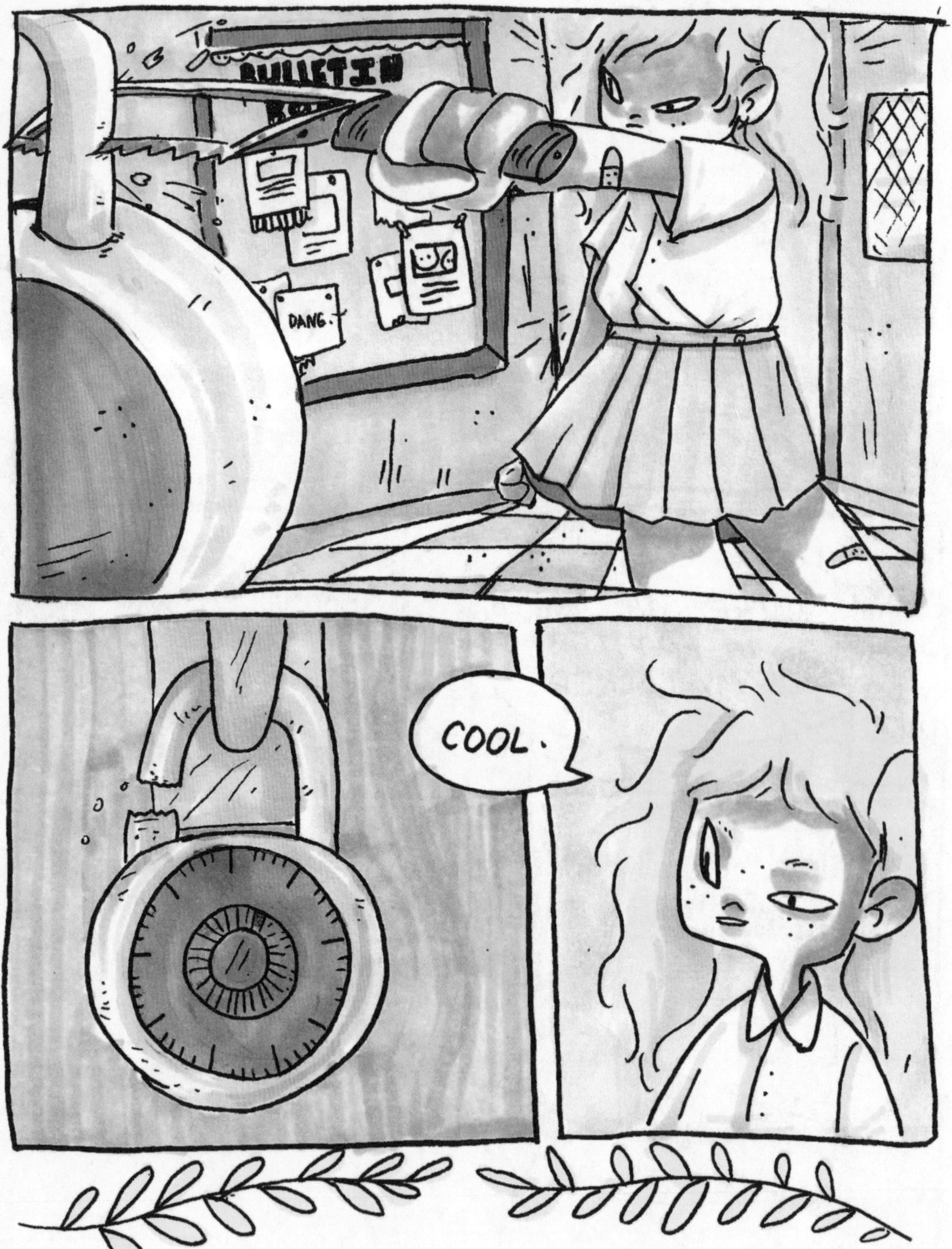
BULLETIN
DANG.
COOL.

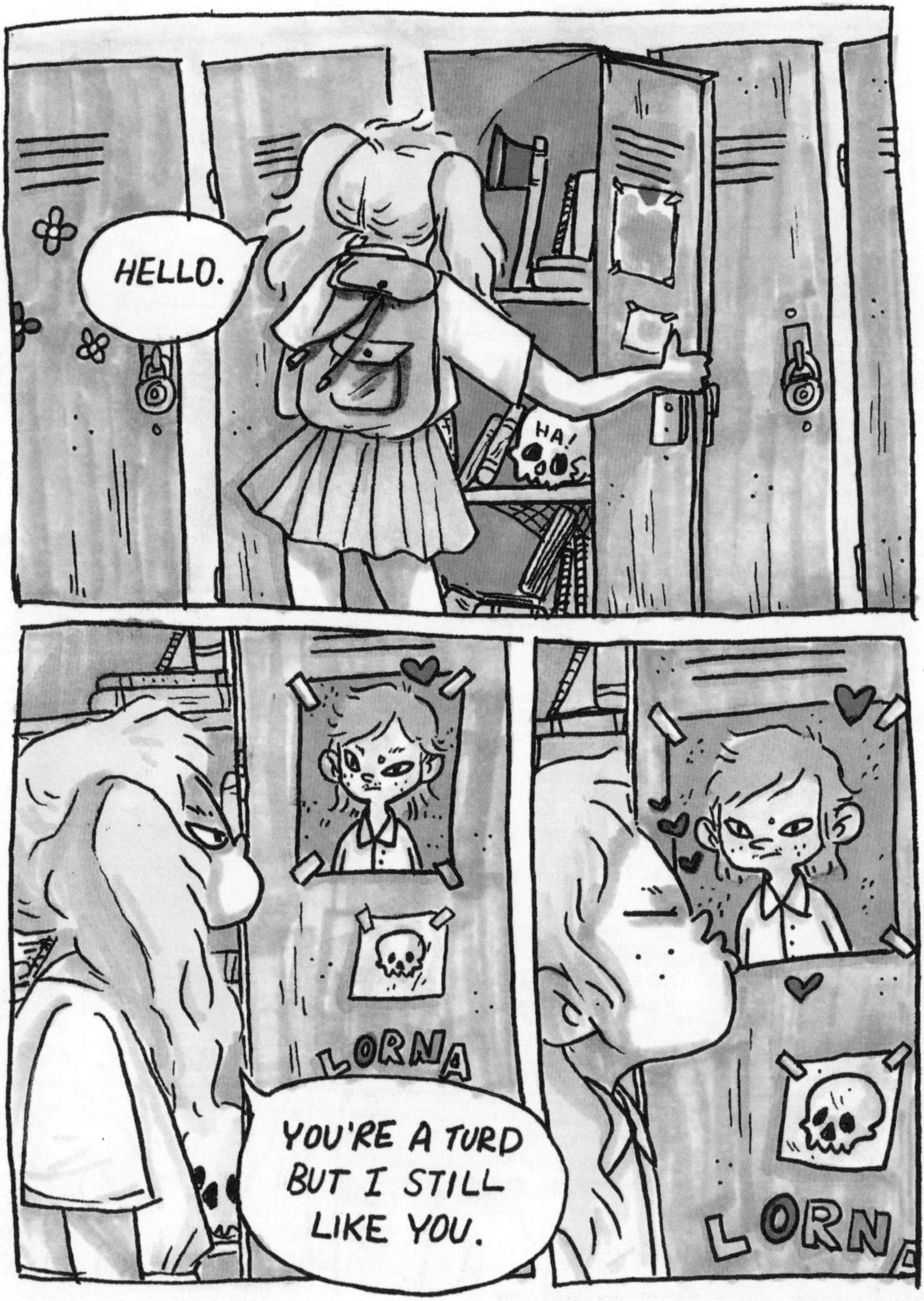
HELLO.
HA!
LORNA
YOU'RE A TURD BUT I STILL LIKE YOU.

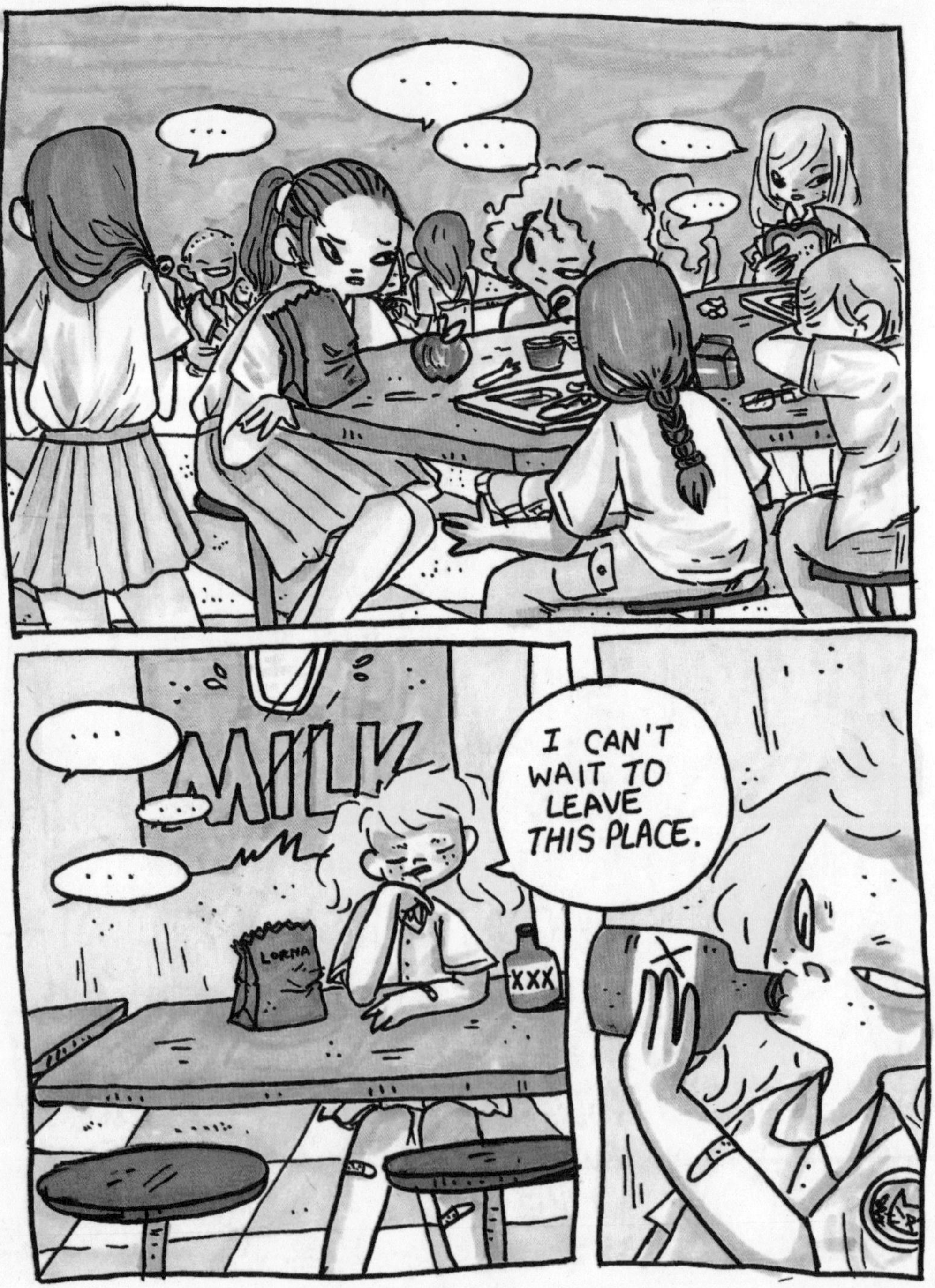
...
...
...
...
...
...
MILK
...
...
LORNA
XXX
I CAN'T WAIT TO LEAVE THIS PLACE.

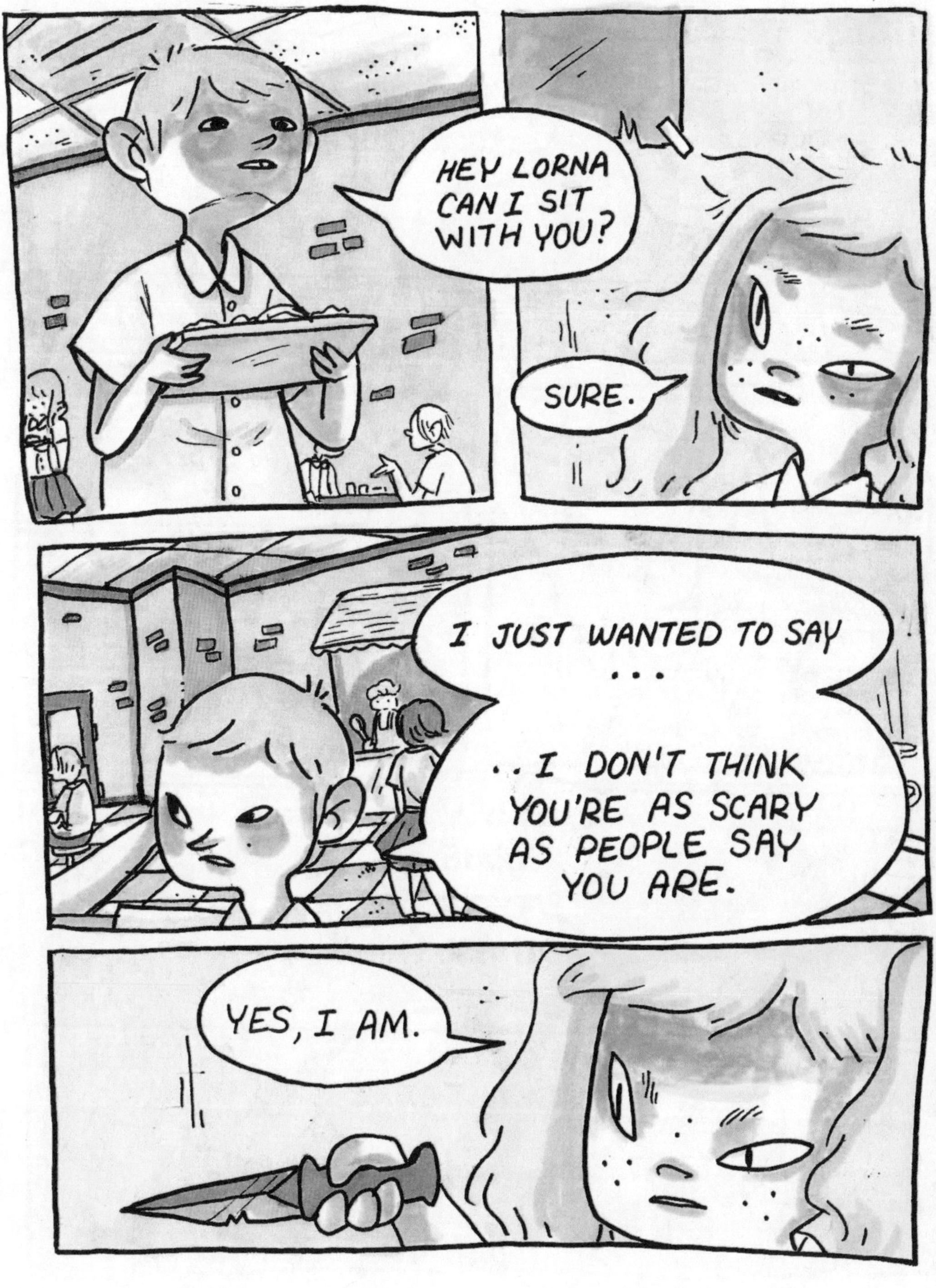
HEY LORNA CAN I SIT WITH YOU?
SURE.
I JUST WANTED TO SAY ...
.. I DON'T THINK YOU'RE AS SCARY AS PEOPLE SAY YOU ARE.
YES, I AM.

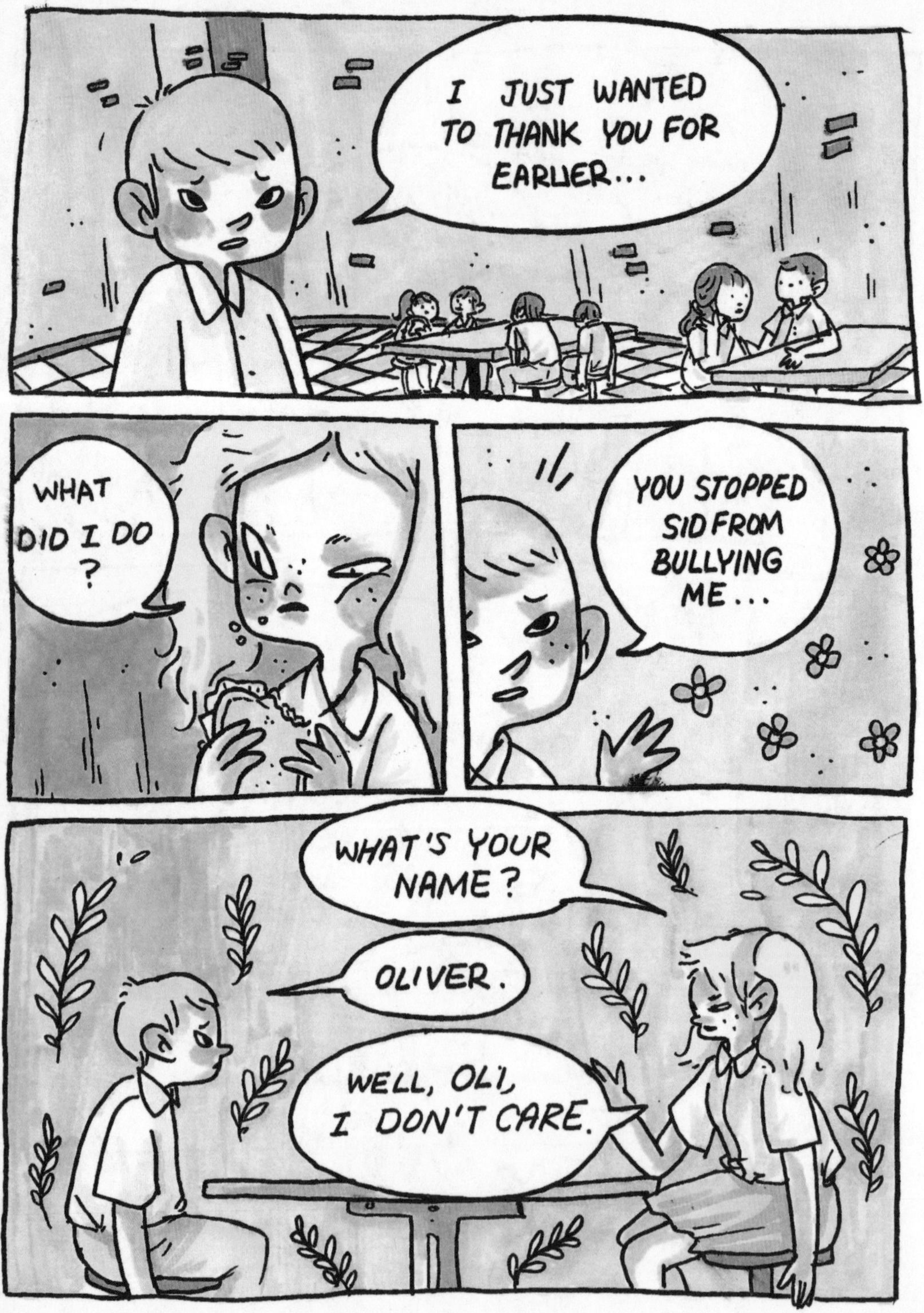
I JUST WANTED TO THANK YOU FOR EARLIER...
WHAT DID I DO ?
YOU STOPPED SID FROM BULLYING ME...
WHAT'S YOUR NAME?
OLIVER.
WELL, OLI, I DON'T CARE.

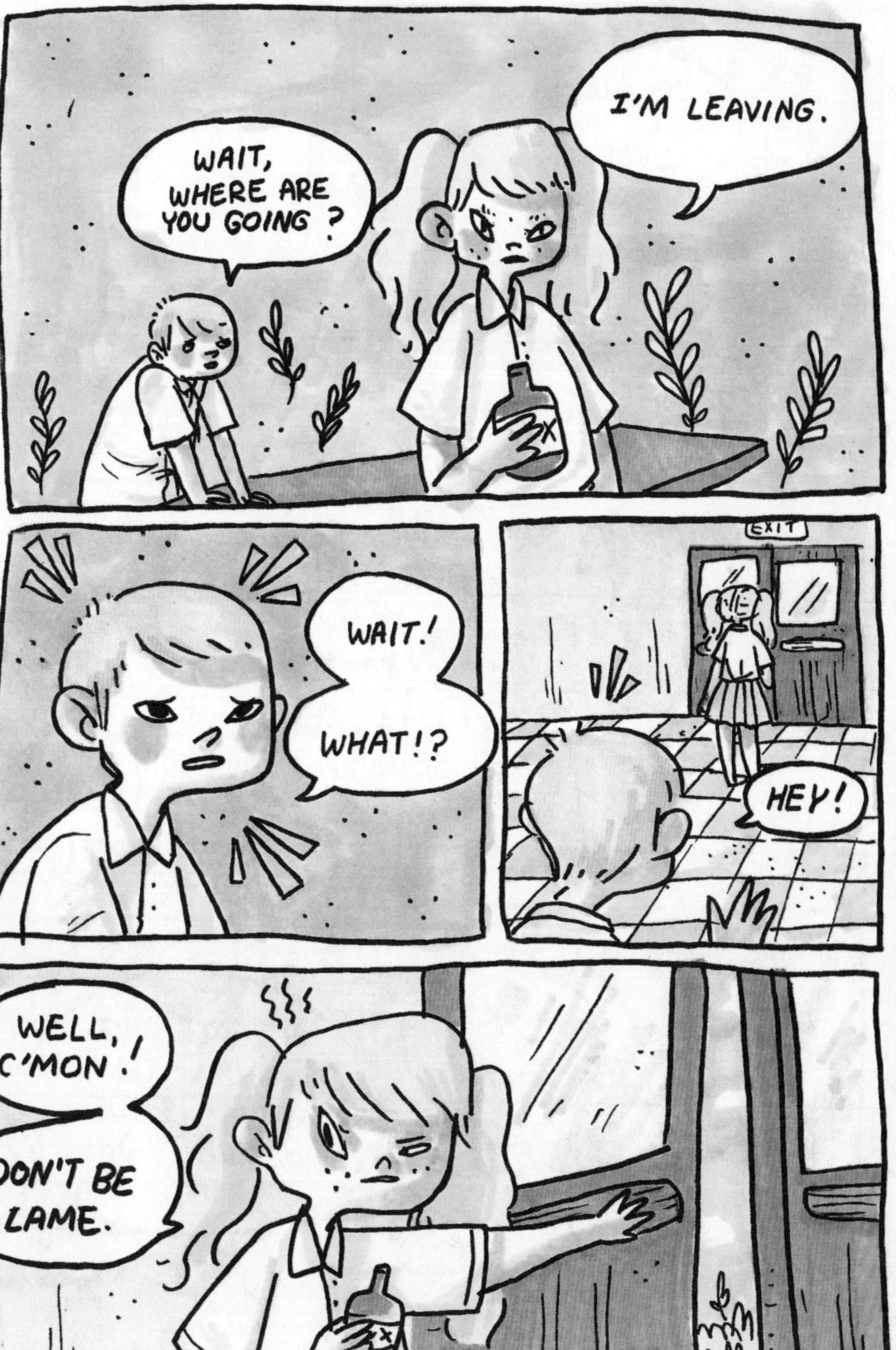
WAIT, WHERE ARE YOU GOING ?
I'M LEAVING.
WAIT!
WHAT!?
EXIT
HEY!
WELL, C'MON!
DON'T BE LAME.

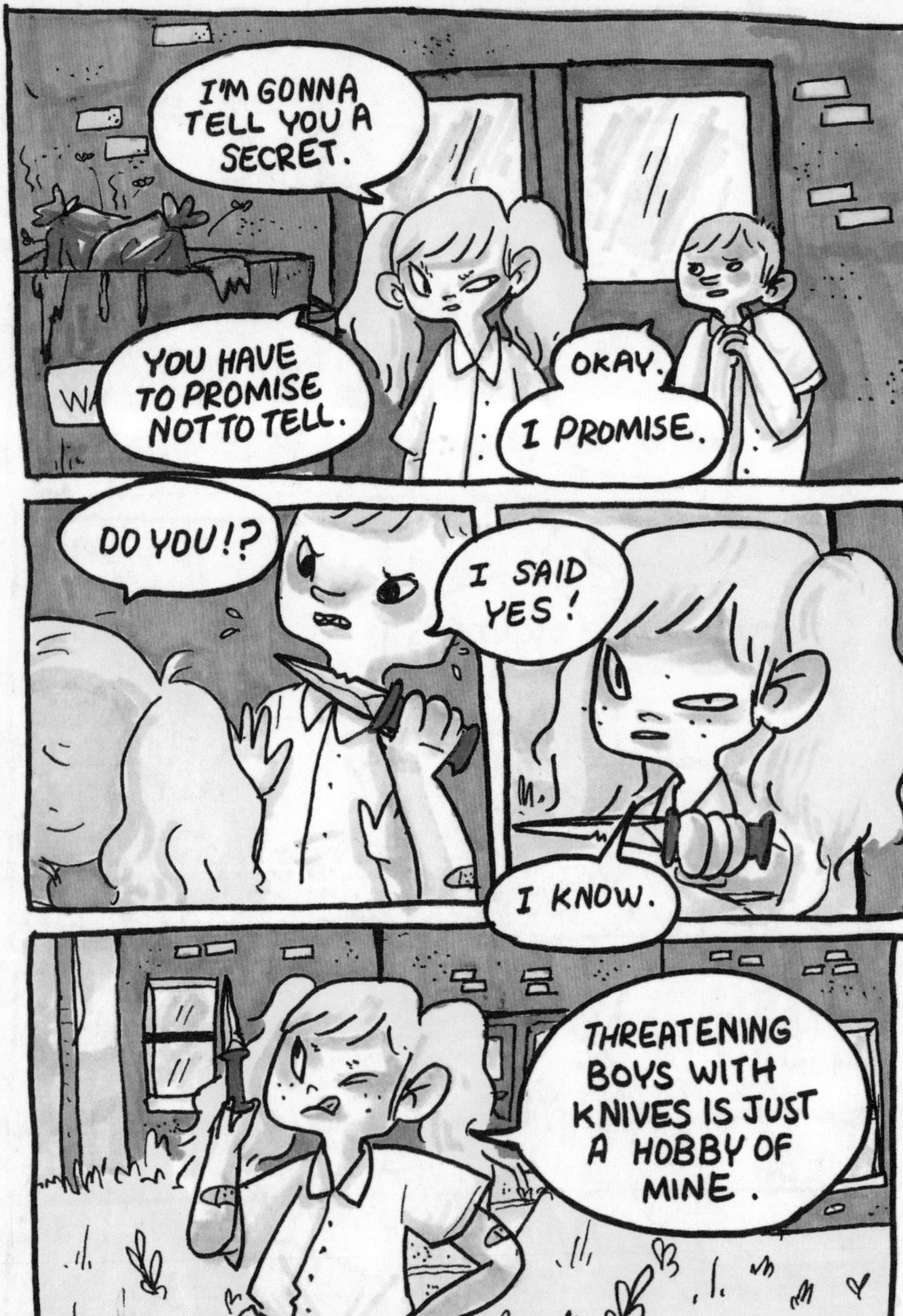
I'M GONNA TELL YOU A SECRET.
YOU HAVE TO PROMISE NOT TO TELL.
OKAY.
I PROMISE.
DO YOU!?
I SAID YES!
I KNOW.
THREATENING BOYS WITH KNIVES IS JUST A HOBBY OF MINE.

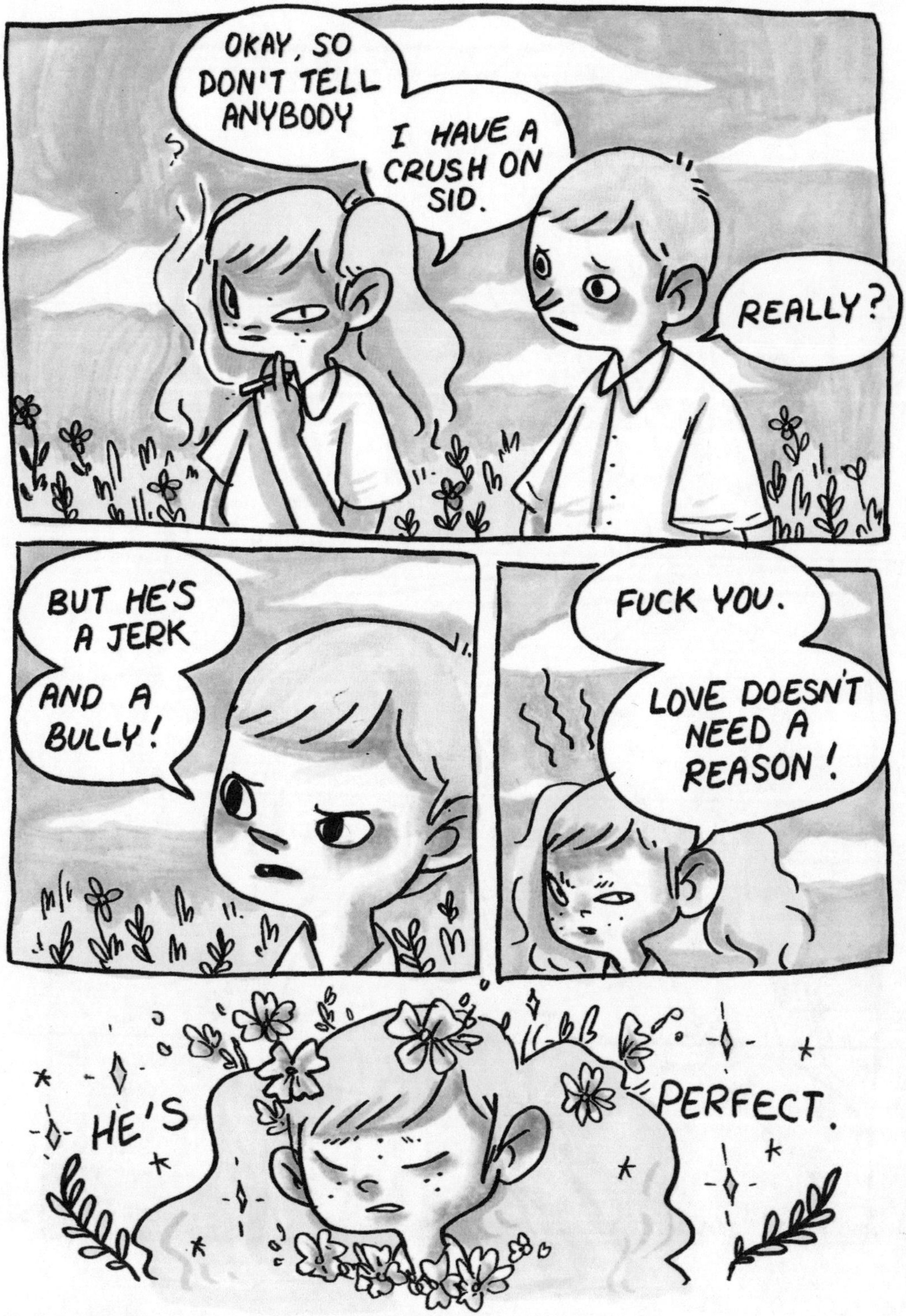
OKAY, SO DON'T TELL ANYBODY
I HAVE A CRUSH ON SID.
REALLY?
BUT HE'S A JERK
AND A BULLY!
FUCK YOU.
LOVE DOESN'T NEED A REASON!
HE'S
PERFECT.

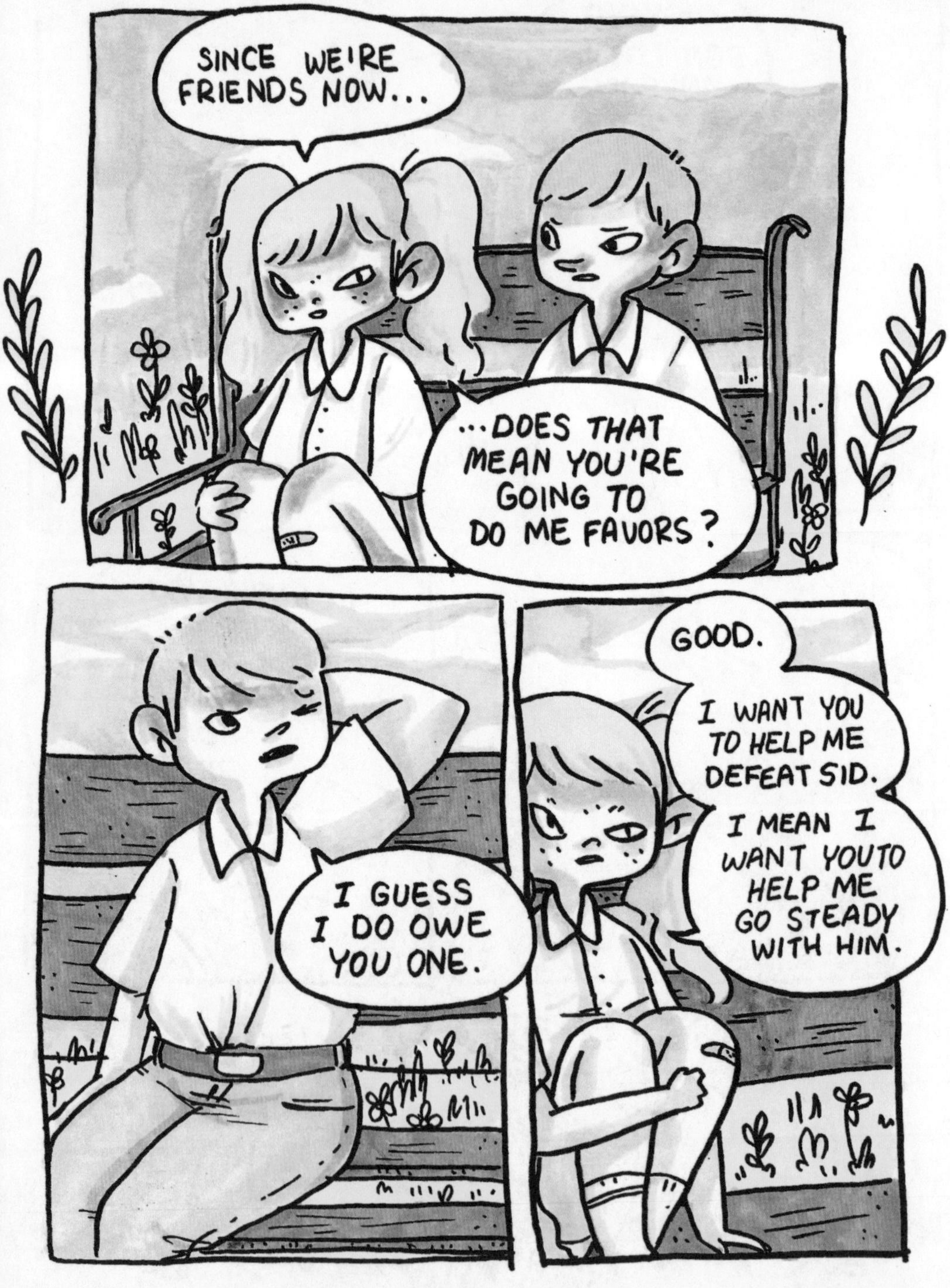
SINCE WE'RE FRIENDS NOW...
...DOES THAT MEAN YOU'RE GOING TO DO ME FAVORS?
I GUESS I DO OWE YOU ONE.
GOOD.
I WANT YOU TO HELP ME DEFEAT SID.
I MEAN I WANT YOU TO HELP ME GO STEADY WITH HIM.

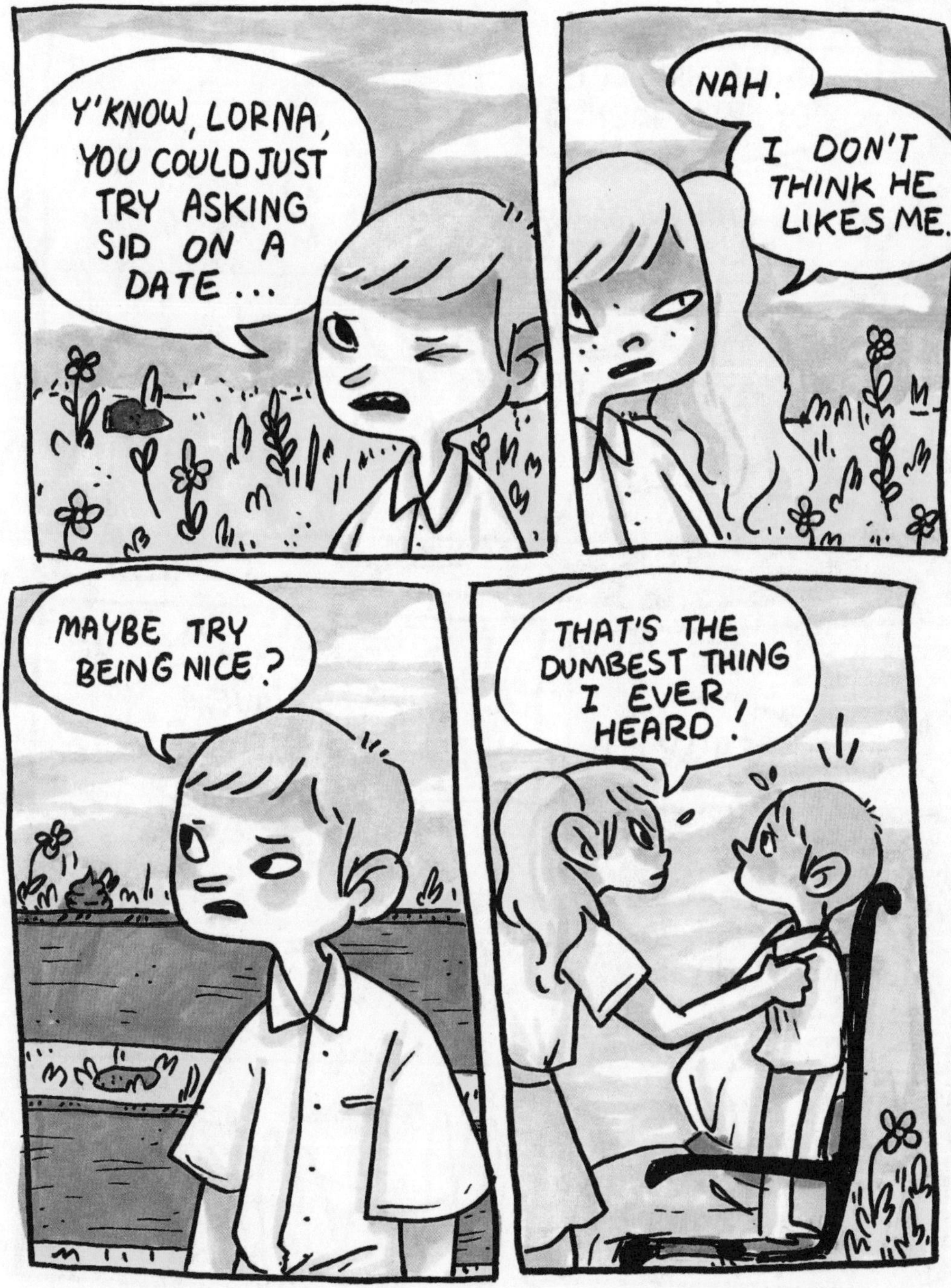
Y'KNOW, LORNA, YOU COULD JUST TRY ASKING SID ON A DATE...
NAH.
I DON'T THINK HE LIKES ME.
MAYBE TRY BEING NICE?
THAT'S THE DUMBEST THING I EVER HEARD!

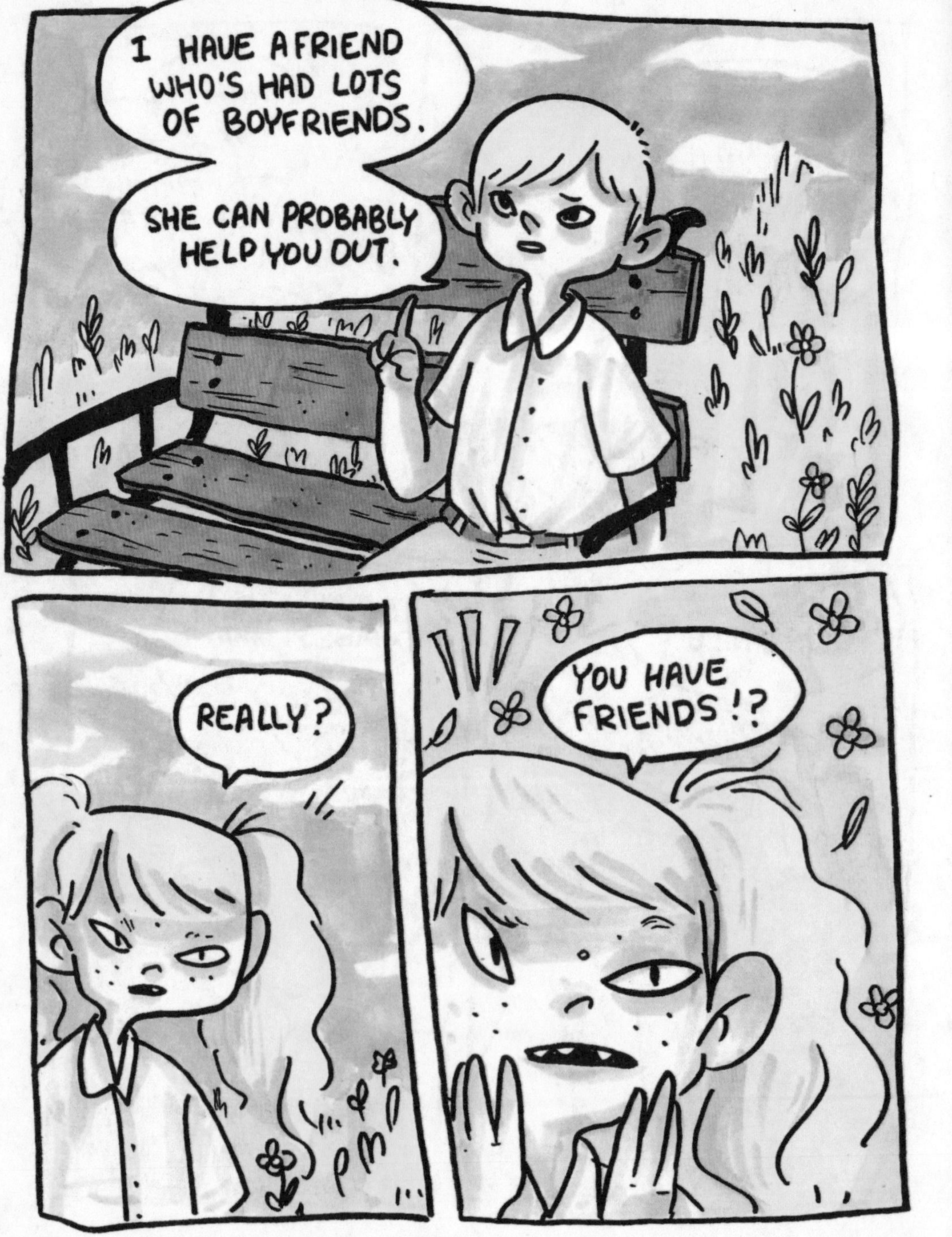
I HAVE A FRIEND WHO'S HAD LOTS OF BOYFRIENDS.
SHE CAN PROBABLY HELP YOU OUT.
REALLY?
YOU HAVE FRIENDS!?

SO, YOU'RE LORNA ?
I HEARD YOU WERE HAVING BOY PROBLEMS.
LORNA, THIS IS NORMA.
WE'VE BEEN NEIGHBORS SINCE, LIKE, SECOND GRADE
SHUT UP, OLIVER.
SO HOW DO I GET A BOY TO LIKE ME?

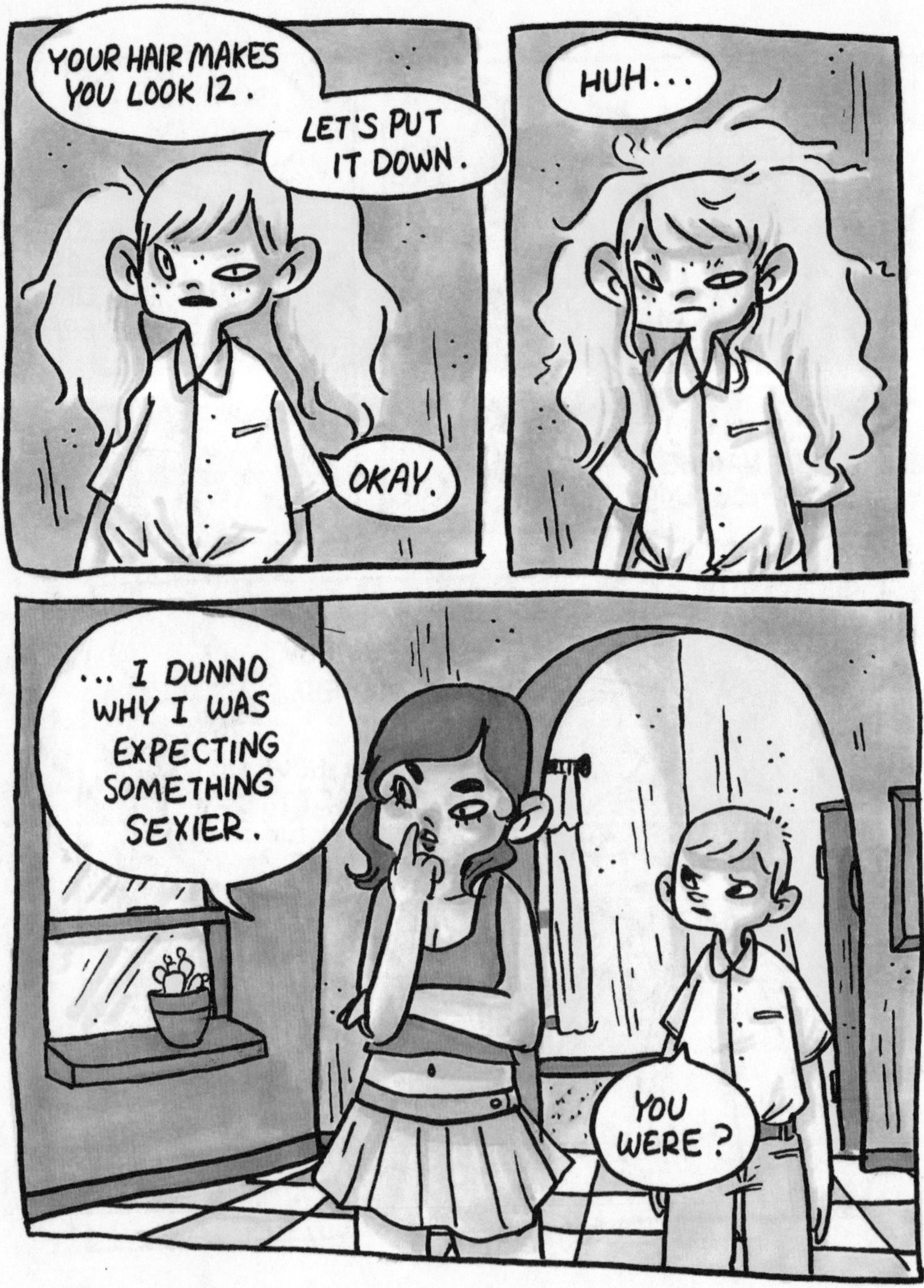
YOUR HAIR MAKES YOU LOOK 12.
LET'S PUT IT DOWN.
OKAY.
HUH...
... I DUNNO WHY I WAS EXPECTING SOMETHING SEXIER.
YOU WERE?

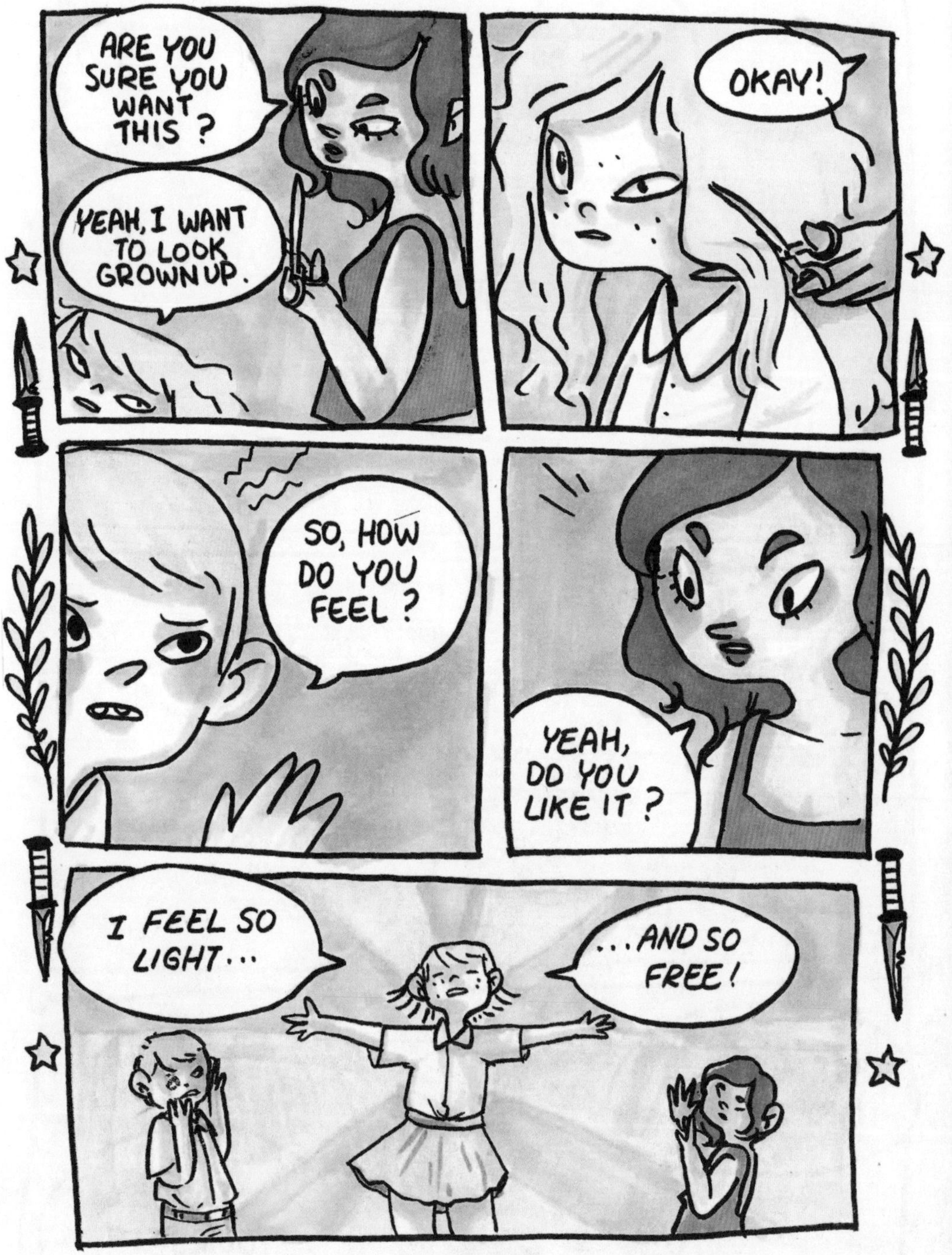
ARE YOU SURE YOU WANT THIS ?
YEAH, I WANT TO LOOK GROWN UP.
OKAY!
SO, HOW DO YOU FEEL ?
YEAH, DO YOU LIKE IT ?
I FEEL SO LIGHT...
...AND SO FREE!

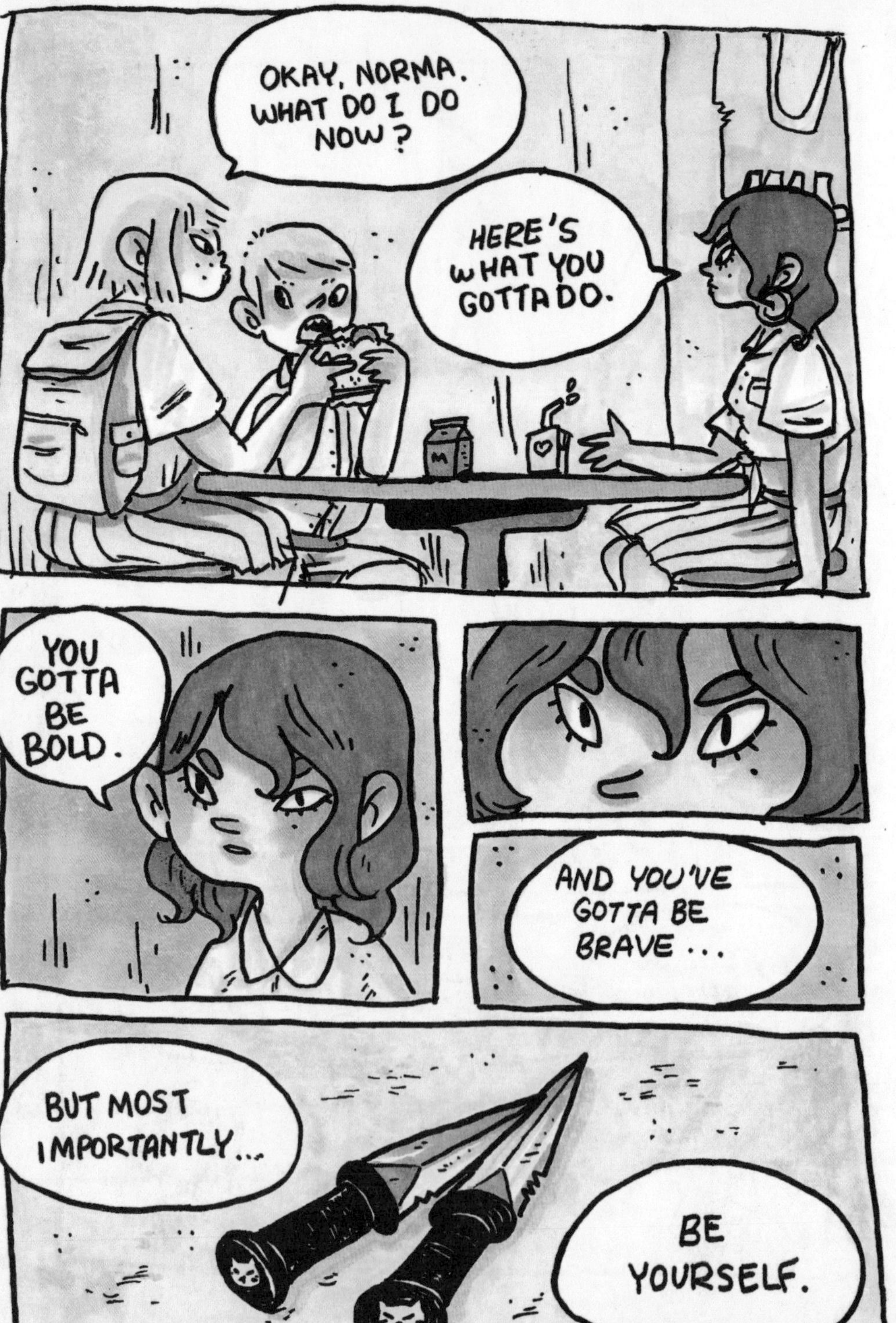
OKAY, NORMA. WHAT DO I DO NOW?
HERE'S WHAT YOU GOTTA DO.
YOU GOTTA BE BOLD.
AND YOU'VE GOTTA BE BRAVE...
BUT MOST IMPORTANTLY...
BE YOURSELF.

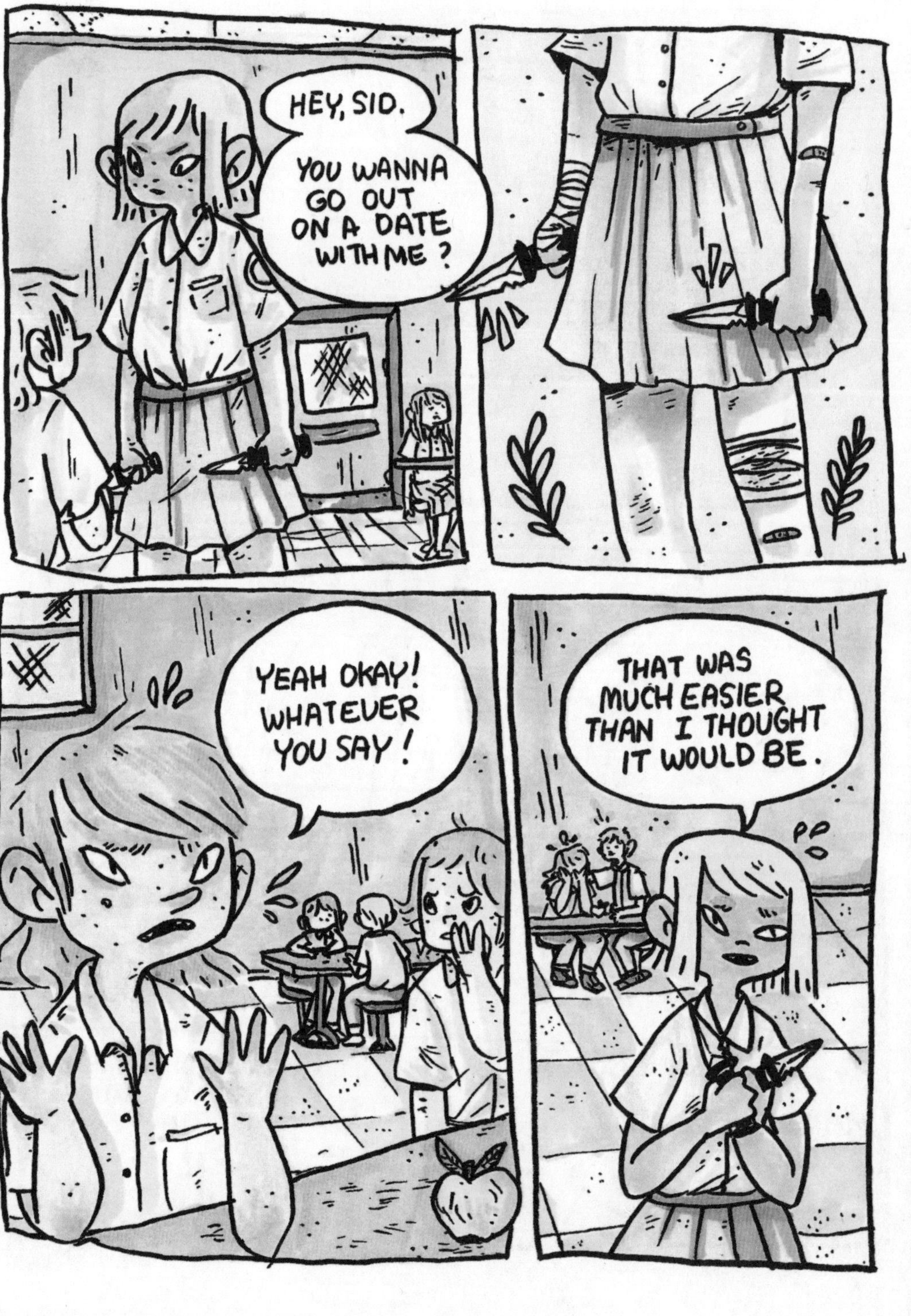
HEY, SID.
YOU WANNA GO OUT ON A DATE WITH ME ?
YEAH OKAY! WHATEVER YOU SAY !
THAT WAS MUCH EASIER THAN I THOUGHT IT WOULD BE .

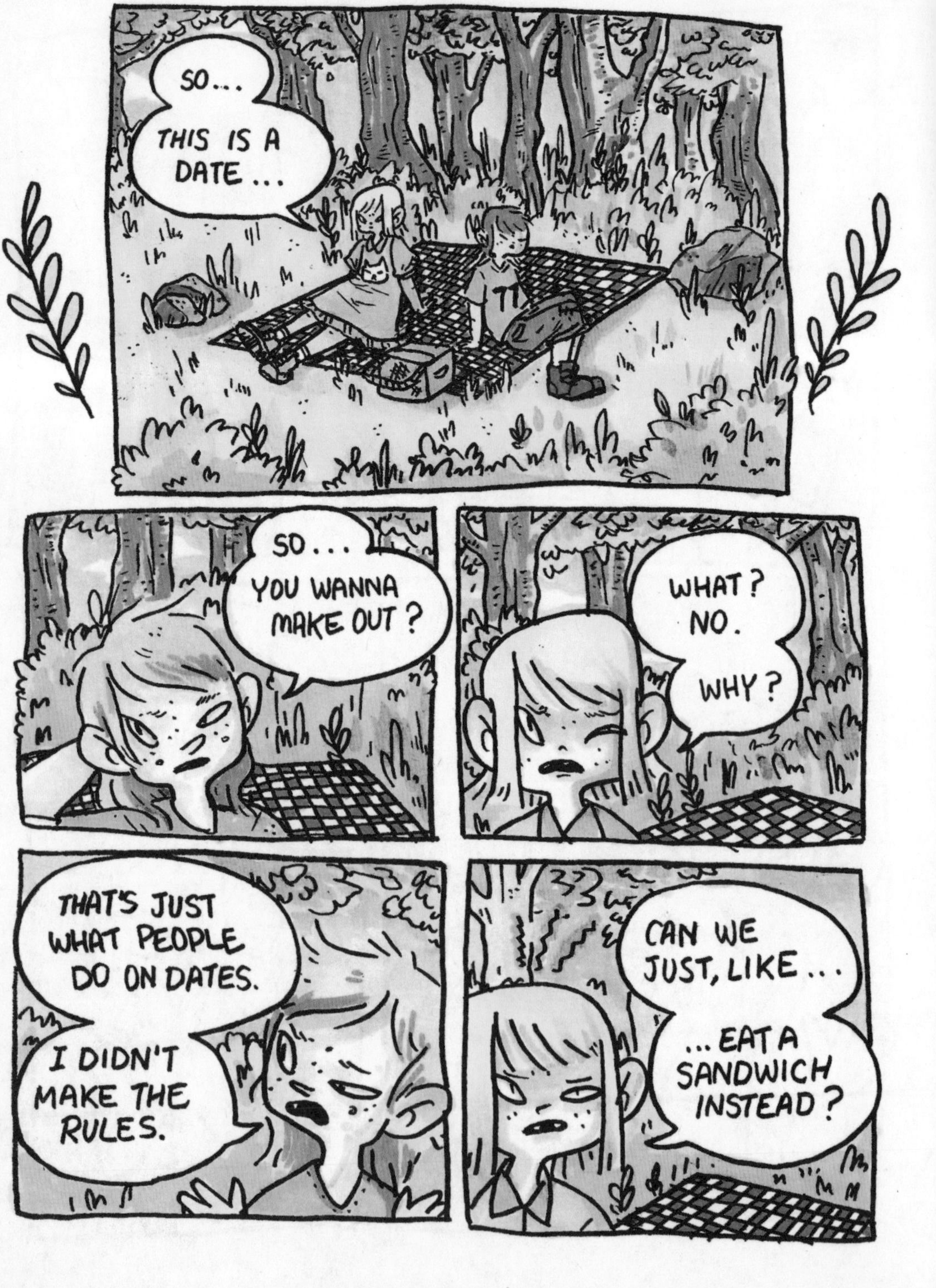
SO....
THIS IS A DATE...
SO... YOU WANNA MAKE OUT?
WHAT? NO.
WHY?
THAT'S JUST WHAT PEOPLE DO ON DATES.
I DIDN'T JUST MAKE THE RULES.
CAN WE JUST, LIKE...
...EAT A SANDWICH INSTEAD?

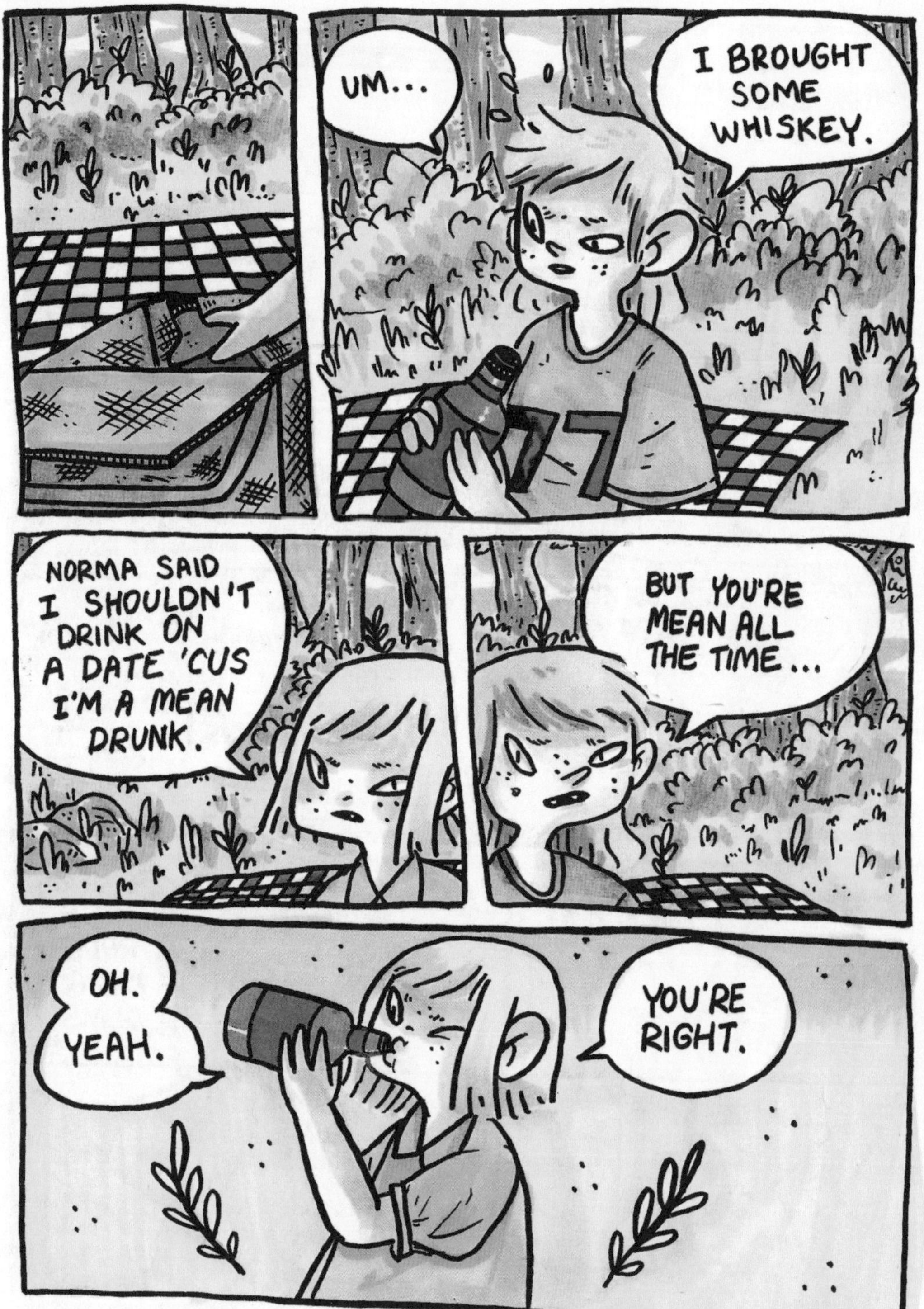
UM...
I BROUGHT SOME WHISKEY.
NORMA SAID I SHOULDN'T DRINK ON A DATE 'CUS I'M A MEAN DRUNK.
BUT YOU'RE MEAN ALL THE TIME...
OH.
YEAH.
YOU'RE RIGHT.

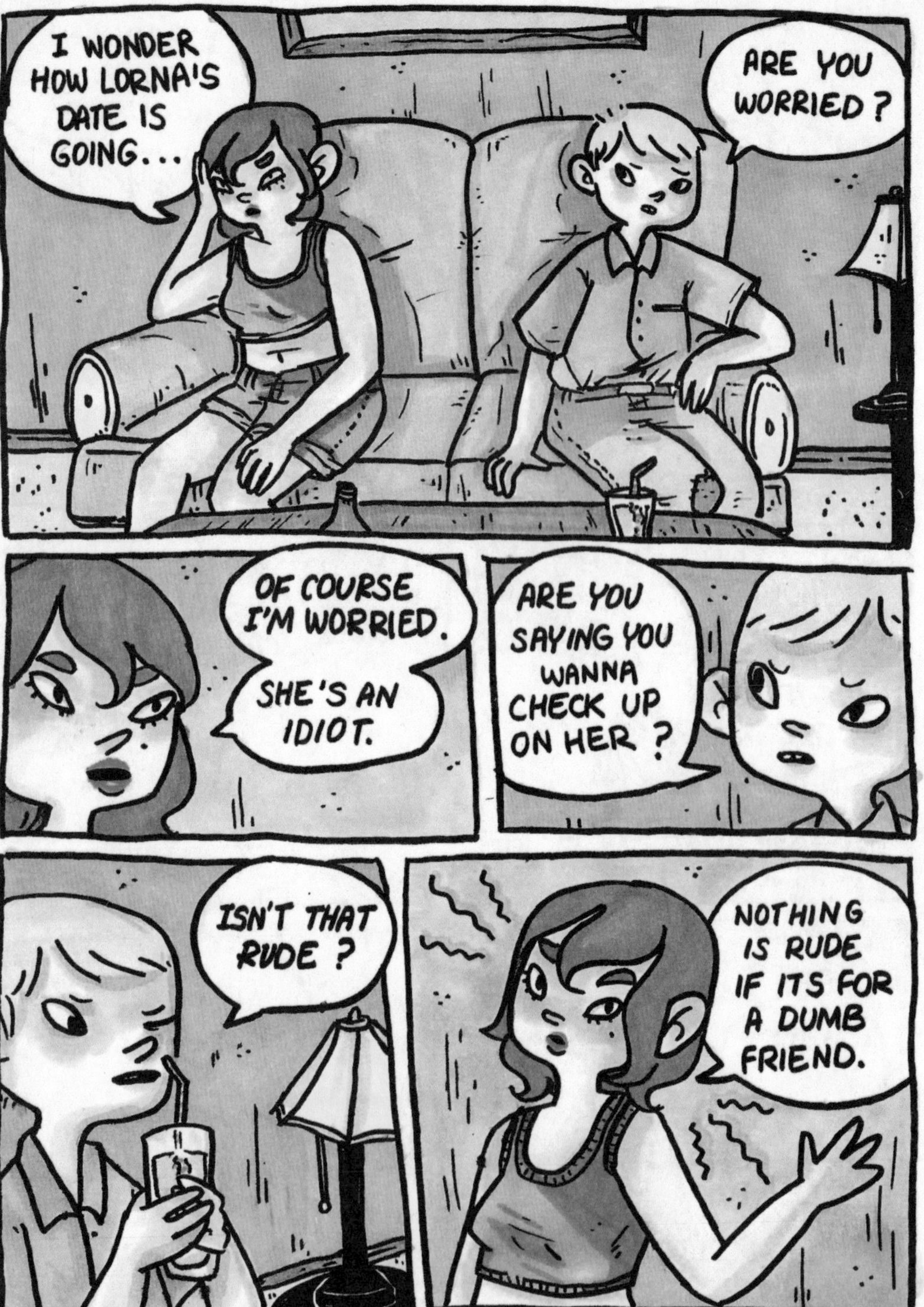
I WONDER HOW LORNA'S DATE IS GOING...
ARE YOU WORRIED?
OF COURSE I'M WORRIED.
SHE'S AN IDIOT.
ARE YOU SAYING YOU WANNA CHECK UP ON HER?
ISN'T THAT RUDE?
NOTHING IS RUDE IF ITS FOR A DUMB FRIEND.

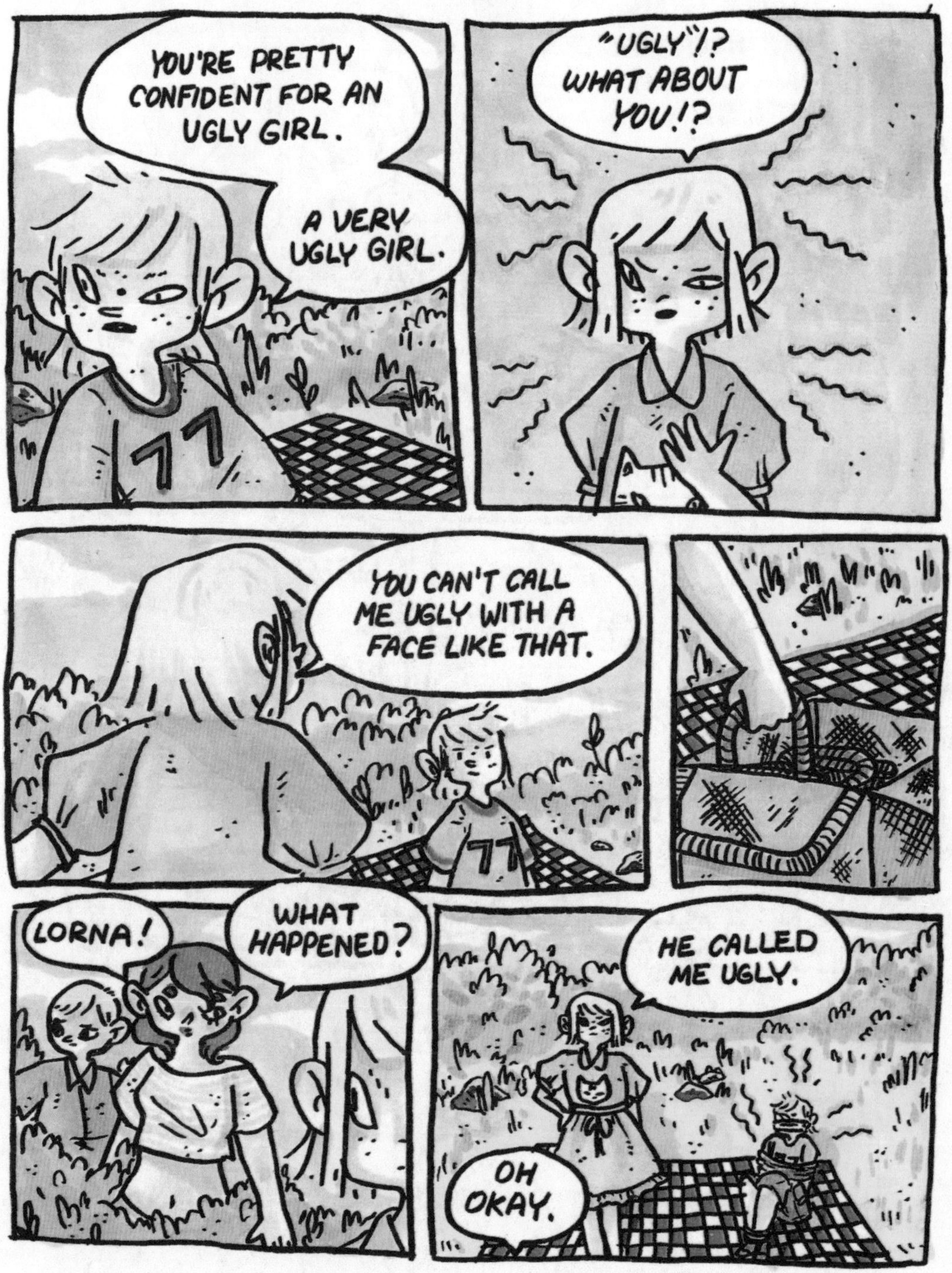
YOU'RE PRETTY CONFIDENT FOR AN UGLY GIRL.
A VERY UGLY GIRL.
"UGLY"!? WHAT ABOUT YOU!?
YOU CAN'T CALL ME UGLY WITH A FACE LIKE THAT.
LORNA!
WHAT HAPPENED?
HE CALLED ME UGLY.
OH OKAY.

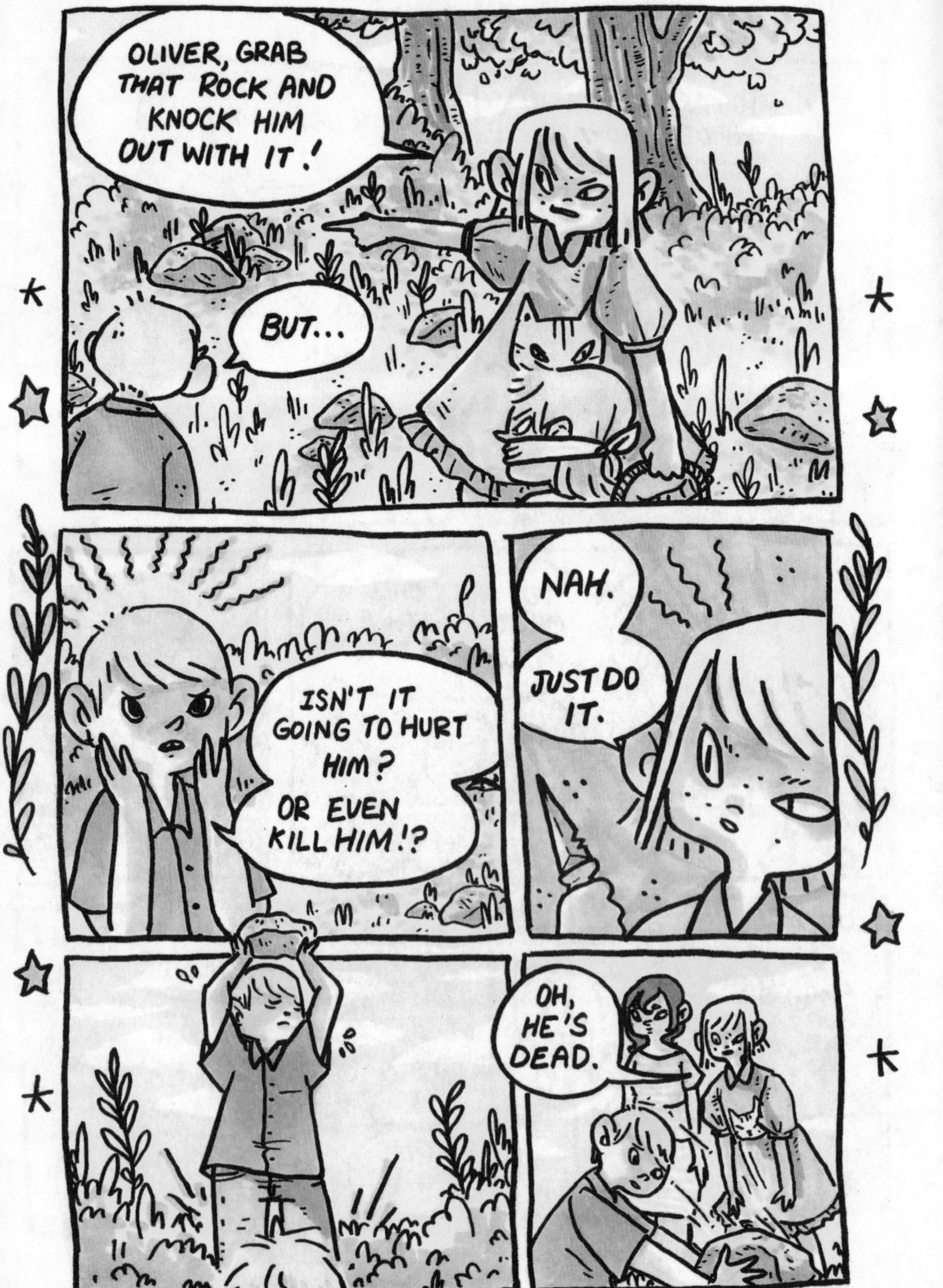
OLIVER, GRAB THAT ROCK AND KNOCK HIM OUT WITH IT!
BUT...
ISN'T IT GOING TO HURT HIM? OR EVEN KILL HIM!?
NAH.
JUST DO IT.
OH, HE'S DEAD.

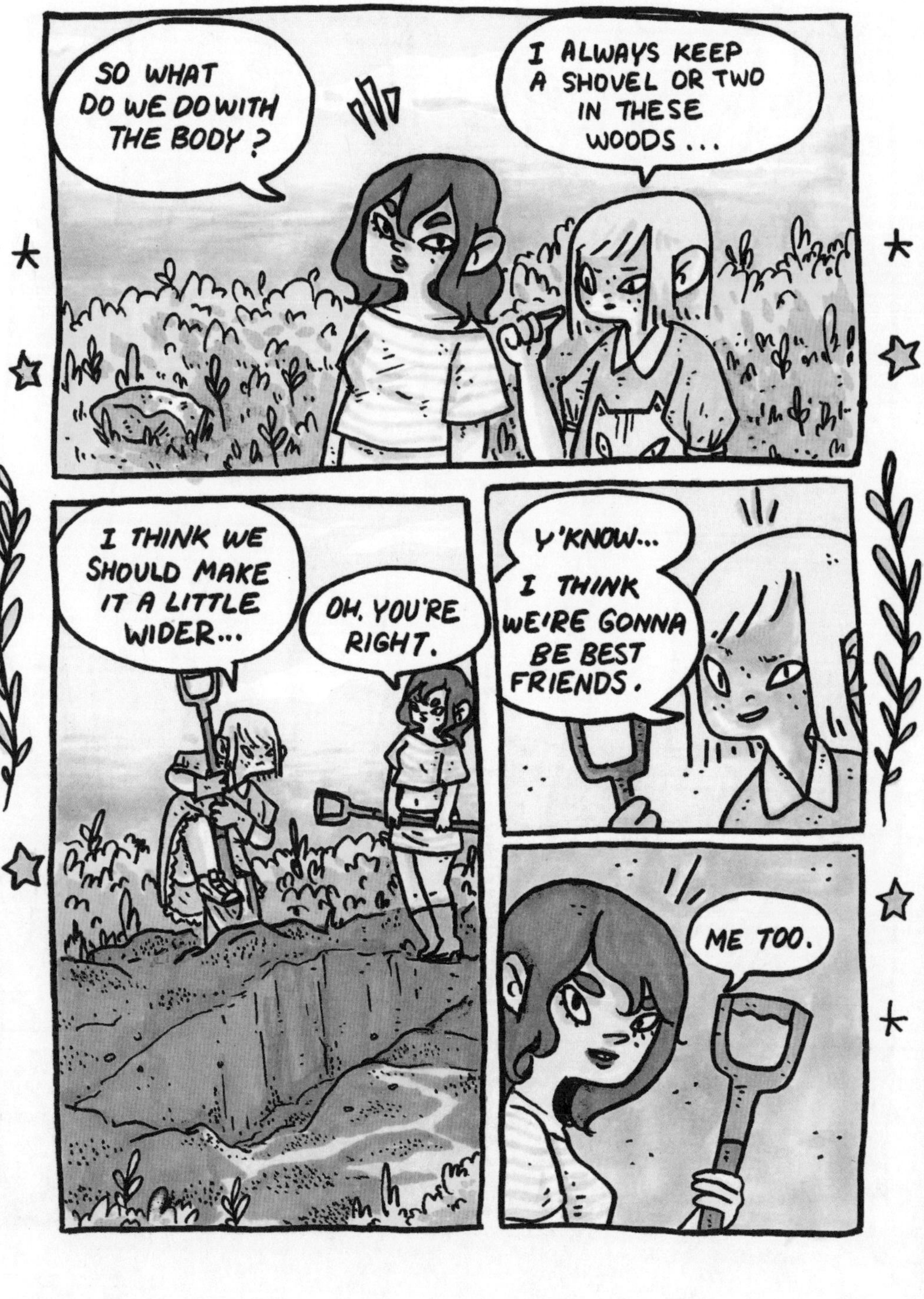
SO WHAT DO WE DO WITH THE BODY?
I ALWAYS KEEP A SHOVEL OR TWO IN THESE WOODS...
I THINK WE SHOULD MAKE IT A LITTLE WIDER...
OH. YOU'RE RIGHT.
Y'KNOW...
I THINK WE'RE GONNA BE BEST FRIENDS.
ME TOO.

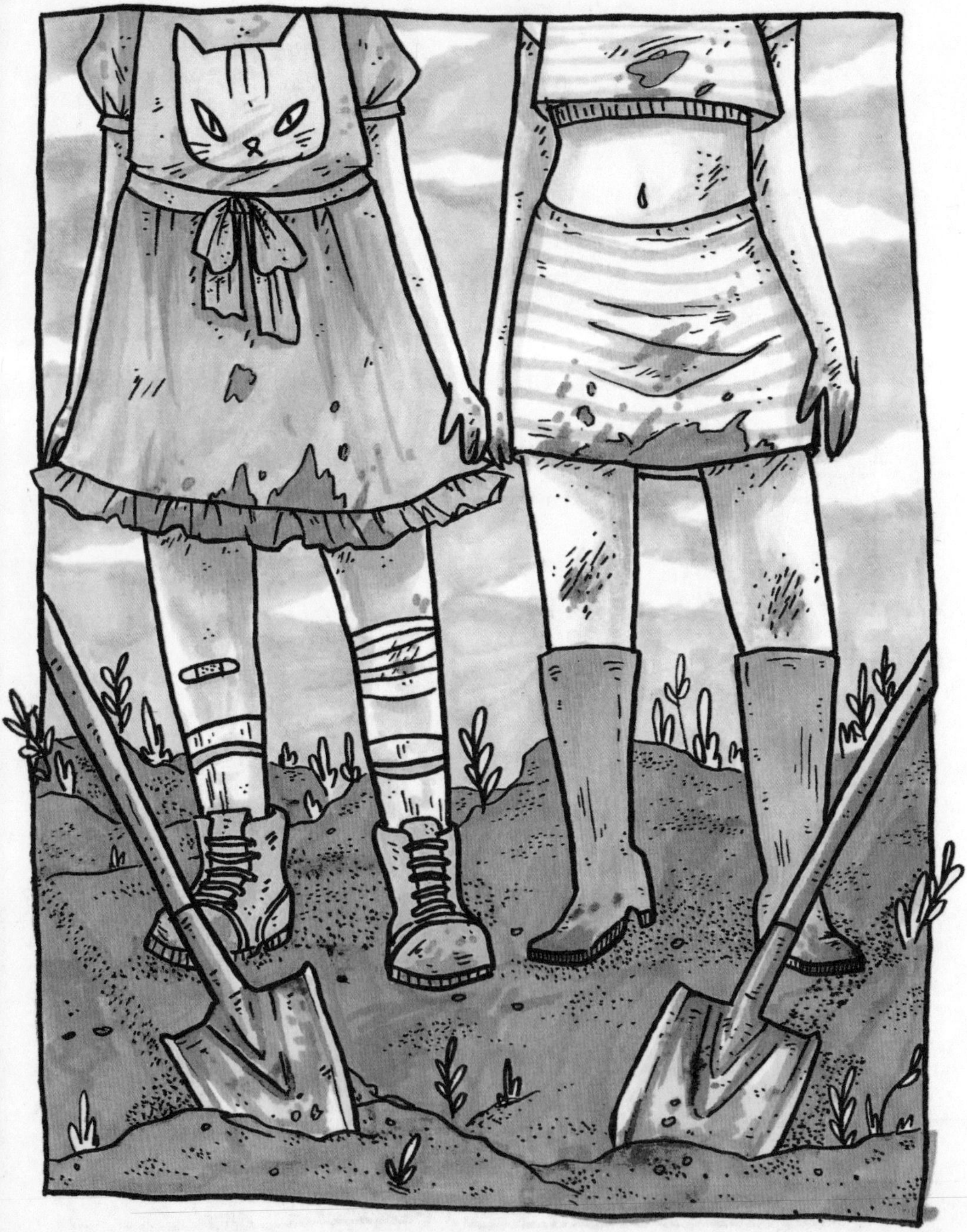

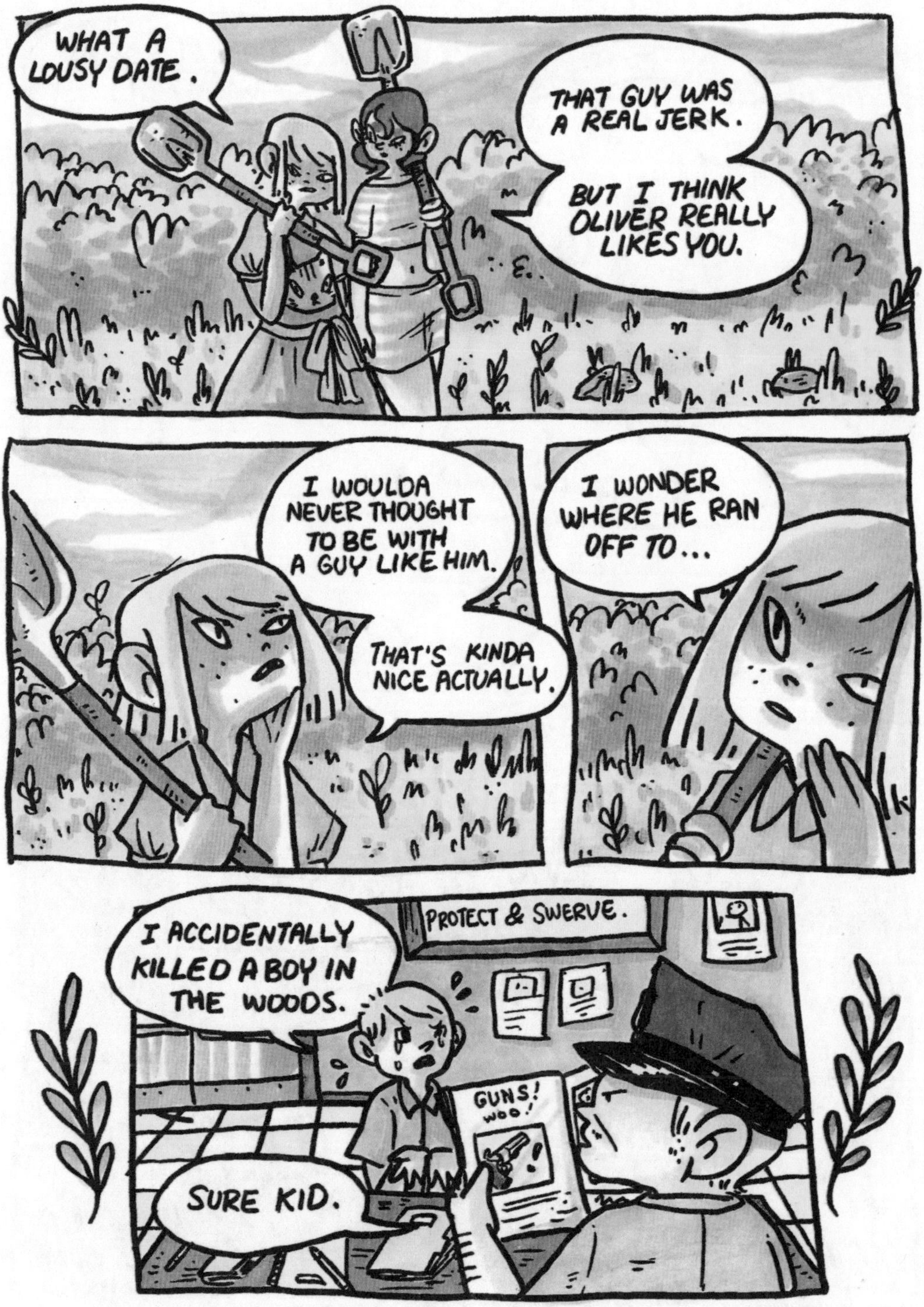
WHAT A LOUSY DATE.
THAT GUY WAS A REAL JERK.
BUT I THINK OLIVER REALLY LIKES YOU.
I WOULDA NEVER THOUGHT TO BE WITH A GUY LIKE HIM.
THAT'S KINDA NICE ACTUALLY.
I WONDER WHERE HE RAN OFF TO...
PROTECT & SWERVE.
I ACCIDENTALLY KILLED A BOY IN THE WOODS.
GUNS! WOO!
SURE KID.

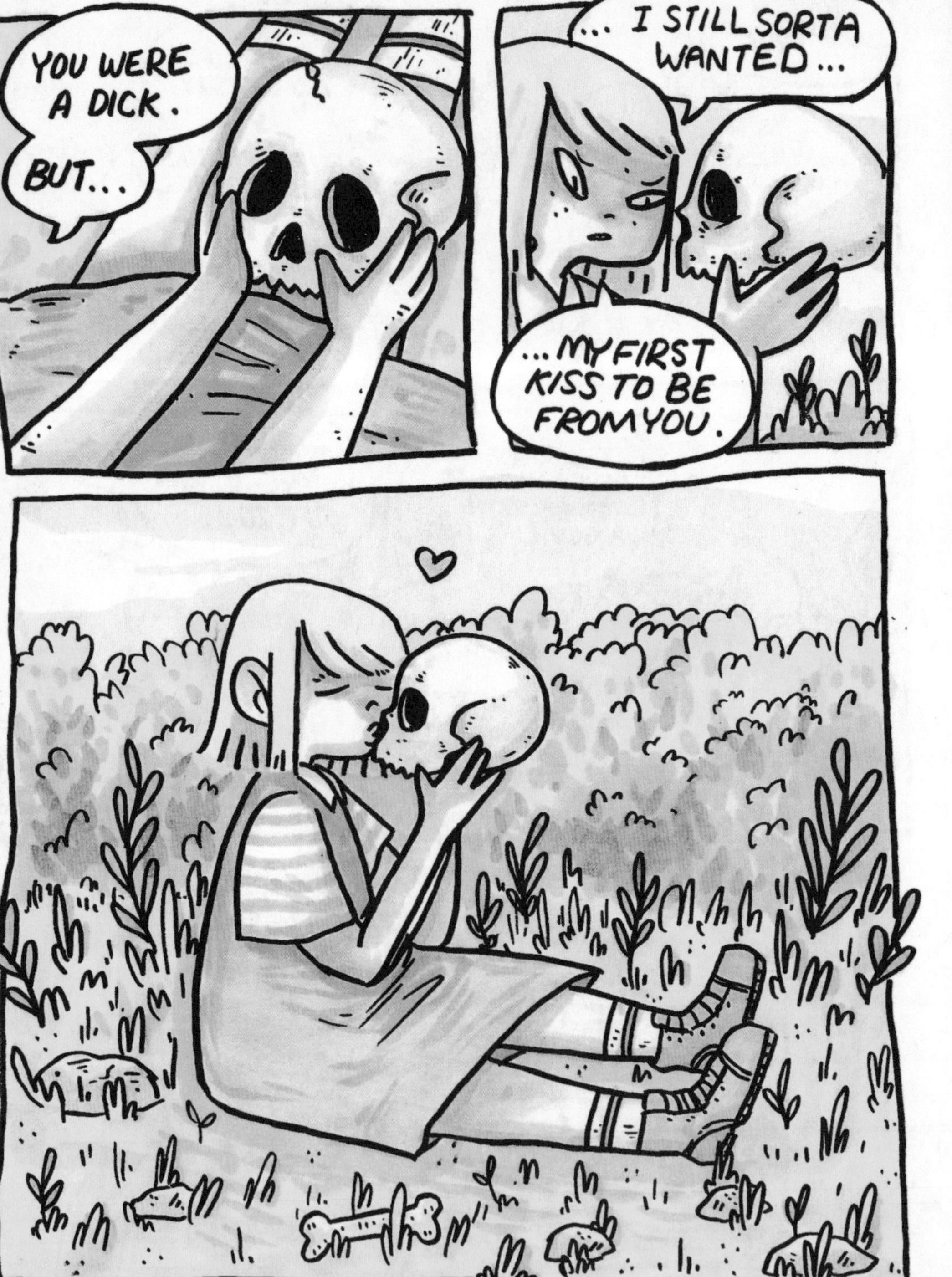
YOU WERE A DICK.
BUT...
... I STILL SORTA WANTED...
... MY FIRST KISS TO BE FROM YOU.

WHAT IS BENJI NATE?

IN NORTH AMERICAN FOLKLORE, BENJI NATE IS
SAID TO BE AN UPRIGHT-WALKING CREATURE
OF SMALL STATURE THAT DWELLS IN
COLLEGE TOWNS AND DRAWS COMICS.

ALLEGED WITNESSES DESCRIBE THE CREATURE AS
LESS THAN FIVE FEET TALL.
NON-THREATENING, ANTISOCIAL, AND
DEFINITELY IN NEED OF A DECENT HAIRCUT.

THE MOST RECENT SIGHTINGS HAVE OCCURRED IN
THE OZARKS WITH HER THREE CATS, ONE DOG,
AND LOVING HUSBAND MICHAEL SWEATER.